Lectionary Worship Aids

Series IX, Cycle B

for the Revised Common Lectionary

by George Reed, O.S.L.

An Anthology of Worship Resources from
The Immediate Word
a Component of **SermonSuite.com**
from CSS Publishing Company

CSS Publishing Company, Inc.
Lima, Ohio

LECTIONARY WORSHIP AIDS, SERIES IX, CYCLE B

FIRST EDITION
Copyright © 2011
by CSS Publishing Co., Inc.

For more information about CSS Publishing Company resources, visit our website at www.csspub.com, email us at csr@csspub.com, or call (800) 241-4056.

ISSN: 1938-7377

ISBN-13: 978-0-7880-2669-0
ISBN-10: 0-7880-2669-0

PRINTED IN USA

*to my wife, Betty,
whose constant love and support has been my greatest joy*

Table of Contents

Music Resources

UMH: United Methodist Hymnal
H82: The Hymnal 1982 (The Episcopal Church)
LBW: Lutheran Book of Worship
PH: Presbyterian Hymnal
CH: Chalice Hymnal
NCH: The New Century Hymnal
NNBH: The New National Baptist Hymnal
AAHH: African-American Heritage Hymnal
CCB: Cokesbury Chorus Book
RENEW: Renew! Songs & Hymns for Blended Worship
ELA: Evangelical Lutheran Worship

Introduction

Early in the history of CSS Publishing Company, we realized that there was a need to provide fresh and relevant worship resources to our customers. Over the years, many different volumes have been developed as an answer to that need. These resources include numerous volumes of *Lectionary Worship Aids*, the *Lectionary Worship Workbook*, and many others.

We live in a world that seems to move faster all the time. Our society continues to react more quickly to the events that go on around us. CSS Publishing has continued to try and fill the need to help pastors relate those current events in their preaching and teaching, thus CSS created a unique service called **The Immediate Word**, an integral part of SermonSuite.com, to assist pastors in tying important news items to God's word. *SermonSuite.com* is a compilation of preaching and worship material that is presented for timely use each week for the parish pastor. The **TIW** team of practicing parish clergy examines current events each week and seeks God's guidance in connecting the assigned lectionary readings with news and current events happening in the world every day. Even though the worship resources were written for a specific time with **TIW**, the writing is relevant for any and every day.

Included in **The Immediate Word** is a worship resource that helps the parish pastor plan for weekly worship. As with previous volumes in this series, this collection contains resources such as calls to worship, hymn selections, and prayers that relate to the lectionary for each week.

This volume contains a collection of these resources for Cycle B of the Revised Common Lectionary that has been gleaned from **The Immediate Word**. It is our prayer that this resource will prove to be an invaluable asset to the success of your ministry.

The editors of CSS Publishing Company, Inc.

Advent 1

Isaiah 64:1-9
1 Corinthians 1:3-9
Mark 13:24-37

Call to Worship
Leader: Hear us, O you who shepherd Israel.
People: You are the One who leads us as a flock.
Leader: Restore us, O God.
People: Come and save us!
Leader: Restore us, O God.
People: Only when you look with favor on us will we be saved.

OR

Leader: Come into the presence of the One who saves us.
People: We are God's people who have waited for God's coming.
Leader: God is coming to save all creation.
People: With joy we welcome our Savior and our God.
Leader: Justice and peace come to all who love our God.
People: This is the day we have awaited. Praise be to God.

OR

Leader: Come into the presence of the Holy One of Israel.
People: Woe to us, for we are a people who are unprepared.
Leader: God comes to mold us into the people we need to be.

People: Woe to us, for we are stiff-necked and hard to work.

Leader: God comes to save us and all creation.

People: Thanks be to God, for we are a people who need to be saved.

Hymns and Sacred Songs
"O Come, O Come, Emmanuel"
found in:
UMH: 211
H82: 56
LBW: 34
PH: 9
CH: 119
NCH: 116
NNBH: 82
AAHH: 188

"Have Thine Own Way, Lord"
found in:
UMH: 382
CH: 588
NNBH: 206
AAHH: 449

"This Is a Day of New Beginnings"
found in:
UMH: 383
CH: 518
NCH: 417

"I Know Whom I Have Believed"
found in:
UMH: 714

"My Lord, What a Morning"
found in:
UMH: 719
PH: 449
CH: 708
NNBH: 499
AAHH: 195

"Wake, Awake, for Night Is Flying"
found in:
UMH: 720
H82: 61/62
LBW: 31

Prayer of the Day / Collect
O God who comes to save your people: Grant us the courage to submit our lives to you so that we may truly know the joy of your salvation; through Jesus Christ our Savior. Amen.

OR

We come into your presence, O God of our salvation, to acknowledge you are the giver of life. We pray that your Spirit will so open our hearts and minds that we will allow you to work the wonders of redemption within and among us. Amen.

Prayer of Confession
Leader: Let us come with humility because of our sins and with confidence because of the love of God to confess our sins to God and in the presence of our sisters and brothers.
People: We confess to you, O God, and in the presence of your people that we have failed to be your faithful people this week. We have done those things that we know we

should not do. We have caused hurt to others and we have offended your great love. We have failed to do those things that you have created us to do. We have left unsaid the words of love and encouragement that you placed in our mouths. We have left undone the acts of love and encouragement that you have placed in our hands.

Forgive us, you who would shape us into your own image as a potter would shape the clay into a vessel good and useful. Awaken us to the ways in which you are coming into the world to save your creation. Fill us once again with your Spirit that we may truly be your children, your image, and the body of our Savior. Amen.

Leader: God desires nothing more than to save the creation through the creatures made from clay. Know that God loves you, forgives you, and empowers you to be the vessel of salvation for all creation.

Prayers of the People (and the Lord's Prayer)

We worship and adore you, O God, for you are the potter and we are but the clay you wish to shape into useful vessels.

(The following may be used if a separate prayer of confession is not used.)

We confess to you, O God, and in the presence of your people that we have failed to be your faithful people this week. We have done those things that we know we should not do. We have caused hurt to others and we have offended your great love. We have failed to do those things that you have created us to do. We have left unsaid the words of love and encouragement that you placed in our mouths. We have left undone the acts of love and encouragement that you have placed in our hands.

Forgive us, you who would shape us into your own image as a potter would shape the clay into a vessel good and useful. Awaken us to the ways in which you are coming into the world to save your creation. Fill us once again with your Spirit that we may truly be your children, your image, and the body of our Savior.

We give you thanks for all the blessings we have received from your hand. We are a people who have been blessed in many ways. You have called us your servants and you have entrusted us with important work. You have invited us to be your image and your presence to all creation. You have entrusted us with your message of salvation.

(Other thanksgivings may be offered.)
We come to you in confidence because of your great love for us and for all of your creation. We offer to you those concerns that rest heavy on our hearts. We offer to you those who suffer in body, mind, or spirit. We offer to you not only the cares of this congregation but also the cares and needs of all the world. We know there are those who feel alone and think that no one cares or prays for them. We ask that you would join our prayers and caring hearts with the prayers and love of our Savior Jesus, who prays for all who are in need. May our spirits join with his and with yours in reaching out in love and care to all who are in need.

All this we ask in the name of our Savior Jesus who taught us to pray always saying:
Our Father... Amen.

(Or if the Our Father is not used at this point in the service)
All this we ask in the name of the Blessed and Holy Trinity. Amen.

Advent 2

Isaiah 40:1-11
2 Peter 3:8-15a
Mark 1:1-8

Call to Worship
Leader: Let us hear what God the Lord will speak,
People: for God will speak peace to the people.
Leader: Surely God's salvation is at hand
People: that God's glory may dwell in our land.
Leader: Righteousness will go before our God
People: and will make a path for God's steps.

OR

Leader: God comes to bring comfort to us.
People: We yearn for God's words of tenderness and love.
Leader: Even in the wilderness God's way will be seen.
People: Through the desert God's road will be straight.
Leader: God comes to gather the lambs to the bosom
People: and to gently lead the mother sheep.

Hymns and Sacred Songs
"Hail to the Lord's Anointed"
found in:
UMH: 203
H82: 616
AAHH: 187
NCH: 104
CH: 140
LBW: 87

"Prepare the Way, O Zion"
found in:
H82: 65
PH: 13
LBW: 26

"Prepare the Way of the Lord"
found in:
UMH: 207
CH: 121

"I Want to Walk as a Child of the Light"
found in:
UMH: 206
H82: 490

"Where Cross the Crowded Ways of Life"
found in:
UMH: 427
H82: 609
PH: 408
NCH: 543
CH: 665
LBW: 429

"Jesu, Jesu"
found in:
UMH: 432
H82: 602
PH: 367
NCH: 498
CH: 600

"*Cuando El Pobre*" ("When the Poor Ones")
found in:

UMH: 434
CH: 662

"Creator of the Earth and Skies"
found in:
UMH: 450
H82: 148
N.B. Second verse:
"We have not known you; to the skies our monuments of folly soar;
and all our self-wrought miseries have made us trust ourselves the more."

"Make Me a Servant"
found in:
CCB: 90

"Walk with Me"
found in:
CCB: 88

"We Are His Hands"
found in:
CCB: 85

Prayer for the Day / Collect
O God who comes in unexpected times, places, and people: Grant us the audacity to believe that you are preparing the way for the kingdom even through the things we do; through Jesus Christ our Lord. Amen.

OR

So often we have been overtaken by events that would seem to crush us whether it has been Pearl Harbor or 9/11

or personal tragedies. Help us to remember that in every event you are there to bring good out of bad, comfort out of distress, salvation out of ruin. Help us to hear again the good news of your care for us in this service and in these scriptures. Amen.

OR

As we come to seek your presence this day, O God, help us to remember those who find it difficult to find your way in their lives. Help us to be aware of the ways that we set barriers before others in the quest for you. Sometimes it is the structure of our buildings, sometimes it is the way we ignore strangers, sometimes it is the way we wish to use them for our gain, and sometimes it is because we just do not see them. Help us to not only see your way but to open it up plainly to others. Amen.

Prayer of Confession

Leader: Our God comes to offer the path of salvation to all creation. Let us confess the ways in which we have failed to walk in that path and the ways we have hindered others from entering it.

People: We confess to you, O God, and before one another that we have sinned in what we have done and in what we have failed to do. We neglected to follow your way in fullness. We are friendly to those we know but we find it hard to welcome strangers into our midst. It makes us uncomfortable and we worry that we make them feel out of place. So we would rather keep them at a distance. We remember all kinds of traditions and practices that we expect others to know and follow but we forget that our Savior told us to "Go into all the world and make disciples of all peoples." Forgive us and direct us back to your path and help us to offer hospitality to everyone.

Leader: God is generous and kind to strangers and to God's children. In the name of God you are forgiven and empowered to live as Christ's disciples, welcoming others into the path of God's life.

Prayers of the People (and the Lord's Prayer)
We adore you and worship you, O God, because you are the very foundation of our existence. Without your breath we would have no life. Yet you are the One who is willing to come to us as a stranger, a slave, or someone in need. You offer us the opportunity to be in communion with you and in service with you in those who are needy around us.

(The following paragraph may be used if a separate prayer of confession has not been used.)
We confess to you, O God, and before one another that we have sinned in what we have done and in what we have failed to do. We neglected to follow your way in fullness. We are friendly to those we know but we find it hard to welcome strangers into our midst. It makes us uncomfortable and we worry that we make them feel out of place. So we would rather keep them at a distance. We remember all kinds of traditions and practices that we expect others to know and follow but we forget that our Savior told us to "Go into all the world and make disciples of all peoples." Forgive us and direct us back to your path and help us to offer hospitality to everyone.

We give you thanks for the hospitality you have offered to us when we were strangers to you and your people. You sought us and called us even when we failed or refused to hear your invitation. You have never rejected us and found us too sinful or too odd to be part of your family.

(Other thanksgivings may be offered.)
We offer to you the brokenness of our lives and of the world.

As you walk about in a stranger's guise, may our love and care join yours in touching the pain and despair of others. May our spirits join yours in holding the creation in loving care. Open our eyes that we may see the places where we can be your physical presence of healing and hope to this world. Open our ears to hear the cries of the lonely and the lost. Open our mouths to speak your gracious words of welcome. Open our arms to bring all into the embrace of your love.

(Other intercessions may be offered.)
All these things we ask in the name of our Savior Jesus Christ who taught us to pray together saying:
Our Father... Amen.

(Or if the Our Father is not used at this point in the service)
All this we ask in the name of the Blessed and Holy Trinity. Amen.

Advent 3

Isaiah 61:1-4, 8-11
1 Thessalonians 5:16-24
John 1:6-8, 19-28

Call to Worship
Leader: When we found ourselves restored by God
People: we were like those who dream.
Leader: God has filled our mouths with laughter
People: and has brought us to shout for joy.
Leader: Restore our fortunes, O God of us all.
People: Let those who have wept now rejoice.

OR

Leader: The Spirit of God is upon us.
People: God has anointed us to bring good news
Leader: to bind up the broken hearted,
People: to proclaim liberty to the captives,
Leader: release to the prisoners,
People: and comfort to those who mourn.

OR

Leader: Come, let us hear what God has to say to us.
People: What word could God have in times like this?
Leader: Let us listen to how God spoke through Isaiah in bad times.
People: What did God say to the people of God back then?
Leader: God sent Isaiah to comfort all who mourn.
People: That is the good news we need from God this day.

Hymns and Sacred Songs

"Come, Ye Disconsolate"
found in:
UMH: 510
AAHH: 421
NNBH: 264
CH: 5021

"Nobody Knows the Trouble I've Seen"
found in:
UMH: 520

"Thou Hidden Source of Calm Repose"
found in:
UMH: 153

"I Will Trust in the Lord"
found in:
UMH: 464
AAHH: 391
NNBH: 285
NCH: 416

"Leaning on the Everlasting Arms"
found in:
UMH: 133
AAHH: 371
NNBH: 262
NCH: 471
CH: 560

"Stand By Me"
found in:
UMH: 512

NNBH: 318
CH: 629

"Out of the Depths I Cry to You"
found in:
UMH: 515
H82: 666
PH: 240
NNBH: 207
NCH: 483
CH: 510
LBW: 295

"I Know Whom I Have Believed"
found in:
UMH: 714

"All My Hope Is Firmly Grounded"
found in:
UMH: 132

"All My Hope on God Is Founded"
found in:
H82: 665
NCH: 408
CH: 88

"All I Need Is You"
found in:
CCB: 100

"On Eagle's Wings"
found in:
Renew: 112

"I Call You Faithful"
found in:
CCB: 70

"Through It All"
found in:
CCB: 61

Prayer for the Day / Collect
O God who has never forsaken your people in any time of trouble: Grant us the faith to hear your words of comfort in this time of mourning for those who are lost and for dreams that are crushed; through Jesus Christ our Savior. Amen.

OR

God, we have come to trust in you. You are the faithful One who has never forsaken your people. We hear the news of the world and it seems so dark and bleak. We doubt if we have the faith to trust that you are with us in these times. We mourn those killed in terror attacks, those taken by disease, and for our dreams that lie shattered at our feet. Comfort us with your Spirit that we may find our hope, once again, in you. Amen.

OR

God of justice and righteousness, in these days of violence and death help us to find our hope in you as the One who is faithful and kind. Help us to offer to you our tear-stained faces that you may wipe them clean with your spirit of joy. Amen.

25

Prayer of Confession

Leader: God has been faithful and has called us to hope in the purposes and intents of our God. Let us confess to God and before one another how we have failed to keep our eyes on our God.

People: We confess to you, our faithful God, and before our sisters and brothers that we have sinned. We have not kept ourselves focused on what God is doing and how God is calling us to be a part of God's claiming all creation. We have let the circumstances of life overwhelm us. We look at the way in which evil seems to abound everywhere and we think there is no redemption for it. We have failed to remember that God has not given up on saving us all. Forgive us and pour out your Spirit upon us that we may believe and act. Amen.

Leader: God desires the salvation of all creation and that includes us. Know that the love and grace of God is abundant and available for you and for all creation. You are the beloved of God.

Prayers of the People (and the Lord's Prayer)

We bring you our worship and praise, O God, because you desire it. Your majesty and glory are beyond our comprehension and we have no way to adequately voice our adoration. But as a parent is blessed by the smallest words of appreciation from a child so you are pleased with our sincere but inadequate praises.

(The following paragraph may be used if a separate prayer of confession has not been used.)

We confess to you, our faithful God, and before our sisters and brothers that we have sinned. We have not kept ourselves focused on what God is doing and how God is calling us to be a part of God's claiming all creation. We have let the circumstances of life overwhelm us. We look at the way in which evil seems to abound everywhere and we think there is no redemption for it. We have failed to remember that God has not given up on saving us all. Forgive us and pour out your Spirit upon us that we may believe and act.

We give you thanks for the way in which you come to redeem all our times. In the midst of tragedy and trouble, you stand holding us and weeping with us and for us. No matter what life brings to us you are there to help us find our way to you and your kingdom.

(Other thanksgivings may be offered.)
We bring to you those who are on our hearts and all who suffer this day. There is much to overwhelm us and cause us to give up hope. By the power of your presence help us all to hope again in that glorious day when Christ shall stand among us and all will be a part of your glorious reign.

(Other intercessions may be offered.)
All these things we ask in the name of our Savior Jesus Christ who taught us to pray together saying:
Our Father... Amen.

(Or if the Our Father is not used at this point in the service)
All this we ask in the name of the Blessed and Holy Trinity. Amen.

Advent 4

2 Samuel 7:1-11, 16
Romans 16:25-27
Luke 1:26-38

Call to Worship
Leader: My soul magnifies the Lord.
People: My spirit rejoices in God my Savior.
Leader: God's mercy is for those who are in awe of our God.
People: God has scattered the proud,
Leader: God has brought down the powerful,
People: God has filled the empty with good things.

OR

Leader: God calls us in humility to come and worship.
People: We stand before God in the truth of who we are.
Leader: We come as sinners who have failed.
People: We come as the image of God who will triumph.
Leader: We come as saints and sinners together.
People: We come as we are to worship our God.

OR

Leader: God invites us to worship the Eternal One.
People: Like David, we want to decide how best to worship.
Leader: God invites us to live under the reign of Christ.
People: Like Mary, we wonder how that can come about.
Leader: God invites us to find joy and life in obedience.
People: Like Mary, let us say, "Yes" to our God and Savior.

Hymns and Sacred Songs

"Tell Out, My Soul"
found in:
UMH: 200
H82: 437/438

"My Soul Gives Glory to My God"
found in:
UMH: 198
CII: 130

"By Gracious Powers"
found in:
UMH: 517
H82: 695/696
PH: 342
NCH: 413

"We Utter Our Cry"
found in:
UMH: 439

"Seek Ye First"
found in:
UMH: 405
H82: 711
PH: 333
CH: 354

Prayer for the Day / Collect

O God who made your servant David to reign as king for your people: Help us to seek to be your faithful servants rather than to be "rulers" over others; through Jesus Christ our Savior. Amen.

OR

O God who made your servant Mary to be the Godbearer for your people: Help us to seek to be your faithful servants rather than to be "rulers" over others; through Jesus Christ our Savior. Amen.

OR

We hear of David and of Mary who were willing to give up their plans in order to be your faithful servants. Help us to hold onto our ambitions a little less tightly and to cling to you more. Amen.

Prayer of Confession

Leader: We have been called to be faithful servants of God. Let us confess to God and before one another the ways in which we have neglected that call.

People: We confess that when we hear the story of David laying aside his plans to build a temple and Mary willingly taking on the task of bearing the Savior, we are not so ready to give up our plans to take on the tasks you set before us, O God. We don't mind serving you when it fits into our plans and fits on our calendars. But when you ask us to give up our time and to serve you by serving the lowly, we find ourselves just a little too busy doing the things that we have decided are important. Help us with Mary and David to listen to your counsel and to be willing to become your faithful servants. Amen.

Leader: God is always ready to receive those who are willing to change and to be changed. Know that God loves you, forgives you, and will give you this week a chance live out your life of service to God more faithfully.

Prayers of the People (and the Lord's Prayer)

We worship and adore you, O God, because you are the One who seeks us out so that we may participate in your great plans for all creation. You call us your children, your friends, your beloved. You call us to be your servants as you take the basin and towel and serve us and others.

(The following paragraph may be used if a separate prayer of confession has not been used.)

We confess that when we hear the story of David laying aside his plans to build a temple and Mary willingly taking on the task of bearing the Savior, we are not so ready to give up our plans to take on the tasks you set before us, O God. We don't mind serving you when it fits into our plans and fits on our calendars. But when you ask us to give up our time to serve you by serving the lowly, we find ourselves just a little too busy doing the things we have decided are important. Help us with Mary and David to listen to your counsel and to be willing to become your faithful servants.

We give you thanks for all the blessings we have received from your bountiful hand. You have given us a creation to play in that is wondrous and beautiful. You have given us one another to love and be loved. You have given us yourself in your Son Jesus Christ.

(Other thanksgivings may be offered.)

The pains, cares, and worries of the world we offer to your great love and kindness. You have given us strength and blessing in the midst of our difficult times, and so we confidently offer those who are on our hearts to you. We know that your love and presence is being offered to them as well.

(Other intercessions may be offered.)

All these things we ask in the name of our Savior Jesus Christ

who taught us to pray together, saying:
Our Father... Amen.

(Or if the Lord's Prayer is not used at this point in the service.)
All this we ask in the name of the Blessed and Holy Trinity.
Amen.

Christmas Eve / Day

Isaiah 9:2-7
Titus 2:11-14
Luke 2:1-14 (15-20)

Call to Worship
Leader: Sing to God a new song!
People: We will tell of God's salvation every day!
Leader: Declare God's glory among the nations!
People: We will tell of God's works to all the peoples!
Leader: Let the heavens be glad and let the earth rejoice!
People: Let the trees of the forest sing for joy!

OR

Leader: God has come among us, let us rejoice!
People: With great joy and singing, we come before God!
Leader: God has come among us, never more to leave!
People: Thanks be to God who dwells among us!
Leader: The Christ has come to share God's love!
People: We are blessed with a God of love and compassion!

Hymns and Sacred Songs
"Angels We Have Heard on High"
found in:
UMH: 238
H82: 96
PH: 23
AAHH: 206
NNBH: 89
NCH: 125

CH: 155
LBW: 71

"Joy to the World"
found in:
UMH: 246
H82: 100
PH: 40
AAHH: 197
NNBH: 94
NCH: 132
CH: 143
LBW: 39

"Love Came Down at Christmas"
found in:
UMH: 242
H82: 84
NCH: 165

"O Morning Star, How Fair and Bright"
found in:
UMH: 247
PH: 69
NCH: 158
CH: 105
LBW: 76

"On this Day Earth Shall Ring"
found in:
UMH: 248
H82: 92
PH: 46

"Silent Night, Holy Night"
found in:
UMH: 239
H82: 111
PH: 60
AAHH: 211
NNBH: 101
NCH: 134
CH: 145
LBW: 65

"That Boy-Child of Mary"
found in:
UMH: 241
PH: 55

"The First Noel"
found in:
UMH: 245
H82: 109
PH: 56
NNBH: 87
NCH: 139
CH: 151
LBW: 56

"All Hail King Jesus"
found in:
CCB: 29
Renew: 35

"Emmanuel, Emmanuel"
found in:
CCB: 31
Renew: 28

Prayer for the Day / Collect

O God who comes into your creation: Grant us the faith to see you among us always that we might discern the presence of the Christ; through Jesus Christ our Savior. Amen.

OR

We have come to worship you, O God, who comes among us as one of us. Your love for us in beyond our understanding and, yet, we rejoice in it all the same. Receive our worship and our praise for you are the One we adore. Amen.

Prayer of Confession

Leader: Let us confess to God and before one another our sins and especially the ways we fail to discern God among us.

People: We confess to you, O God, and before one another that we have sinned. You have come among us to dwell with and within us and yet we are so often unaware of your loving presence. You walk beside us and we feel alone. You offer your love and guidance and we feel lost. Forgive us and open our eyes to see the glory of your incarnation not only in the créche but all around us each day. Amen.

Leader: God has come among us to heal us and bring us salvation. Know that God loves us and forgives us and offers us the power of God's own Spirit to restore us to wholeness.

Prayers of the People

We praise you for your glorious power that is seen in the humble birth of a baby in a stable.

(The following paragraph may be used if a separate prayer of confession has not been used.)

We confess to you, O God, and before one another that we have sinned. You have come among us to dwell with and within us and yet we are so often unaware of your loving presence. You walk beside us and we feel alone. You offer your love and guidance and we feel lost. Forgive us and open our eyes to see the glory of your incarnation not only in the crèche but all around us each day.

We give you thanks for your presence among us and for this holy sign whereby you have come into our world.

(Other thanksgivings may be offered.)
We offer to you the hurts and cares of your world that you have come to in order to bring salvation and wholeness to it. Help us, as the body of Christ, to make the incarnation known every day.

(Other intercessions may be offered.)
All these things we ask in the name of our Savior Jesus Christ who taught us to pray together saying:
Our Father... Amen.

(Or if the Our Father is not used at this point in the service)
All this we ask in the name of the Blessed and Holy Trinity. Amen.

Christmas 1

Isaiah 61:10—62:3
Galatians 4:4-7
Luke 2:22-40

Call to Worship
Leader: Praise God! Praise God from the heavens!
People: Praise God, all you angels, all you hosts!
Leader: Let all creation praise our God,
People: for God commanded and they were created.
Leader: Young men and women, old and young alike,
People: praise the Lord!

OR

Leader: Once we were no people.
People: But now we are the people of God!
Leader: Once we were without identity.
People: But now God has adopted us as children!
Leader: Once we had no future.
People: But now we are the heirs of God with Christ!

OR

Leader: When people curse us,
People: we will bless them.
Leader: When people call us bad names,
People: we will call them children of God.
Leader: When people won't associate with us,
People: we will open our hearts and doors to them.

Hymns and Sacred Songs

"It Is Well with My Soul"
found in:
UMH: 377
AAHH: 377
NNBH: 255
NCH: 438
CH: 561

"I Will Trust in the Lord"
found in:
UMH: 464
AAHH: 391
NNBH: 285
NCH: 416

"Lead Me, Lord"
found in:
UMH: 473
AAHH: 145
NNBH: 341
CH: 593

"How Firm a Foundation"
found in:
UMH: 529
H82: 636/637
AAHH: 146
NNBH: 48
NCH: 407
CH: 618
LBW: 507

"Be Still, My Soul"
found in:

UMH: 534
AAHH: 135
NNBH: 263
NCH: 488
CH: 566

"Filled with the Spirit's Power"
found in:
UMH: 537
NCH: 266
LBW: 160

"The Church's One Foundation"
found in:
UMH: 545/546
H82: 525
PH: 442
AAHH: 337
NNBH: 297
NCH: 386
CH: 272
LBW: 369

"In Christ There Is No East or West"
found in:
UMH: 548
H82: 529
PH: 439/440
AAHH: 398/399
NCH: 394/395
CH: 687
LBW: 359

"I Am Thine, O Lord"
found in:

UMH: 419
AAHH: 387
NNBH: 202
NCH: 455
CH: 601

"Wash, O God, Our Sons and Daughters"
(although meant for infant baptism, this hymn has great identity themes)
found in:
UMH: 605
AAHH: 674
CH: 365

"This Is the Spirit's Entry Now"
(another baptismal hymn, but what better speaks of our identity?)
found in:
UMH: 608
LBW: 195

"Something Beautiful"
found in:
CCB: 84

"We Are His Hands"
found in:
CCB: 85

Prayer for the Day / Collect
O God who created us in your own image: Grant us the courage to accept that our identity is based in you and give us the grace to live out the lofty name you have called us; through Jesus Christ our Savior. Amen.

OR

You have called us by our true name, God, and have created us and gifted us with all we need to live up to the name. Help us as we praise your name and hear your word that we may accept our identity in you. Amen.

Prayer of Confession

Leader: God our Creator is the One who knows us and names us. Let us confess to God and before one another how we have accepted as our identity what others say about us.

People: God, we have sinned against you and before our sisters and brothers. We have been given an identity in you that rises us up beyond all creation. We have been adopted by you and called your very own children. You have placed in us the Spirit of Jesus so that he has become our elder brother. And yet we view ourselves as having little worth or we think our worth depends on the things we have done or that we own. We have forgotten that you are our Creator and our Parent who loves us and calls us by our true name. Forgive our foolish ways and by the power of your Spirit inspire us to live out our identity in you for all to see so that they may know they too are your children. Amen.

Leader: You are God's children and God will never abandon you or forsake you. In the name of Christ, you are forgiven. Amen.

Prayers of the People (and the Lord's Prayer)

We worship and adore you, O God, because you are not only the creator of the ends of the universe but also because you have created us. You have made us in your image and given your very own Spirit to us. You are the great One who comes to claim us as your very own children.

(The following paragraph may be used if a separate prayer of confession has not been used.)

God, we have sinned against you and before our sisters and brothers. We have been given an identity in you that rises us up beyond all creation. We have been adopted by you and called your very own children. You have placed in us the Spirit of Jesus so that he has become our elder brother. And yet we view ourselves as having little worth or we think our worth depends on the things we have done or that we own. We have forgotten that you are our Creator and our Parent who loves us and calls us by our true name. Forgive our foolish ways and by the power of your Spirit inspire us to live out our identity in you for all to see so that they may know they too are your children. Amen.

We give you thanks for all the ways you have blessed us as your children. You have given us a beautiful creation, which supplies our needs and is filled with beauty and wonder that feeds our souls. You have given us the love and care of family and friends. You have given us a place in your church and made us part of your holy family.

(Other thanksgivings may be offered.)

We offer up to your loving care those who are on our hearts today. We are aware that many live without knowing you as God, Creator, Parent, and Friend. We know that many allow themselves to be named by others or by their diseases or by their circumstances. As you move among them and call them by their true name, may we be aware of how we can be your presence and call people the Beloved in your name.

(Other intercessions may be offered.)

All these things we ask in the name of our Savior Jesus Christ who taught us to pray together, saying:
Our Father... Amen.

(Or if the Lord's Prayer is not used at this point in the service.)
All this we ask in the name of the Blessed and Holy Trinity. Amen.

New Year's Day

Ecclesiastes 3:1-13
Revelation 21:1-6a
Matthew 25:31-46

Call to Worship
Leader: O God, our Sovereign, how majestic is your name in all the earth!
People: You have set your glory above the heavens.
Leader: When I look at your heavens, the work of your fingers,
People: the moon and the stars that you have established;
Leader: what are we that you are mindful of us
People: yet you have crowned us with glory and honor.
Leader: You have given us dominion over the works of your hands.
People: O God, our Sovereign, how majestic is your name in all the earth!

OR

Leader: Our times are in the hands of our God.
People: Let us rejoice that our lives are secure in God.
Leader: We don't know what the future holds
People: But we know that our God holds our future.
Leader: Let us begin this year in the praise and worship of God.
People: This day and all days belong to our God!

Hymns and Sacred Songs
"I Am Thine, O Lord"
found in:

UMH: 419
AAHH: 387
NNBH: 202
NCH: 455
CH: 601

"O Master, Let Me Walk with Thee"
found in:
UMH: 430
H82: 659/660
PH: 357
NNBH: 445
NCH: 503
CH: 602
LBW: 492
ELA: 818

"This Is a Day of New Beginnings"
found in:
UMH: 383
NCH: 417
CH: 518

"Spirit of the Living God"
found in:
UMH: 393
PH: 322
AAHH: 320
NNBH: 133
NCH: 283
CH: 259
Renew: 90

"Praise to the Lord, the Almighty"
found in:

UMH: 139
H82: 390
AAHH: 117
NNBH: 2
NCH: 22
CH: 25
ELA: 858/859
Renew: 57

"Great Is Thy Faithfulness"
found in:
UMH: 140
AAHH: 158
NNBH: 45
NCH: 423
CH: 86
ELA: 733
Renew: 249

"Dear Lord, Lead Me Day by Day"
found in:
UMH: 413

"A Charge to Keep I Have"
found in:
UMH: 413
AAHH: 467/468
NNBH: 436

"Shine, Jesus, Shine"
found in:
CCB: 81
Renew: 247

"Great Is the Lord"
found in:
CCB: 65
Renew: 22

Prayer for the Day / Collect

O God who was and is and ever shall be: Grant us who are mortal and bound by time the grace to number the days and apply ourselves to the wisdom that leads to life eternal; through Jesus Christ our Savior. Amen.

OR

We come to worship you, O God, the Eternal One who is beyond the limits of time. As we praise your name and hear your word, grant us the wisdom to follow our Savior Jesus this day and throughout this new year. Amen.

Prayer of Confession

Leader: Let us confess to God and before one another our sins and especially our failure to seize the day of our salvation.

People: We confess to you, O God, and before one another that we have sinned. We live our daily lives as if we were immortal. We put off the truly important things that pertain to the very depths of our souls while we are distracted by the trivial and the silly. We spend more time worrying about what we will wear than we do thinking about who we are and who you are calling us to become. Forgive our tunnel vision that can only see what is right before us and misses the wide vistas of your love. Amen.

Leader: Our salvation is God's constant work. God waits only for us to turn and allow that sweet redeeming work to take place in our lives. Know that God is here and hears us whenever we seek God's presence.

Prayers of the People (and the Lord's Prayer)

We worship and bless your name, O God, for your timeless love and care for creation. You are in our lives in the midst of all our activities seeking our salvation.

(The following paragraph may be used if a separate prayer of confession has not been used.)

We confess to you, O God, and before one another that we have sinned. We live our daily lives as if we were immortal. We put off the truly important things that pertain to the very depths of our souls while we are distracted by the trivial and the silly. We spend more time worrying about what we will wear than we do thinking about who we are and who you are calling us to become. Forgive our tunnel vision that can only see what is right before us and misses the wide vistas of your love.

We give you thanks for all the opportunities you have in store for us in the coming year. We thank you for your faithfulness in the year that is past. We thank you for the opportunity to give ourselves once more to you and to your service.

(Other thanksgivings may be offered.)

We pray for your creation and for your saving help that you bring to it. We pray that we may be faithful in being part of your saving presence to those around us in the year to come.

(Other intercessions may be offered.)

All these things we ask in the name of our Savior Jesus Christ who taught us to pray together saying:
Our Father... Amen.

(Or if the Our Father is not used at this point in the service)

All this we ask in the name of the Blessed and Holy Trinity. Amen.

Epiphany of Our Lord

Isaiah 60:1-6
Ephesians 3:1-12
Matthew 2:1-12

Call to Worship
Leader: Arise, shine; for your light has come,
People: and the glory of God has risen upon us.
Leader: Lift up your eyes and look around;
People: your sons and daughters shall come from far away.
Leader: Then you shall see and be radiant and
People: our hearts shall thrill and rejoice.

OR

Leader: Come and draw near to the light of God.
People: If we come to God's light, God will see our sin.
Leader: God already knows who we are and God loves us.
People: If we come to God's light, we will see our sin.
Leader: God accepts us even when we can't accept ourselves.
People: With trust in God's grace, we will come to the light of the world.

Hymns and Sacred Songs
"Christ, Whose Glory Fills the Skies"
found in:
UMH: 173
H82: 6/7
PH: 462/463
LBW: 265

"When Morning Gilds the Skies"
found in:
UMH: 185
H82: 427
PH: 487
AAHH: 186
NCH: 86
CH: 100
LBW: 545/546

"O Zion, Haste"
found in:
UMH: 573
H82: 539
NNBH: 422
LBW: 397

"We Three Kings"
found in:
UMH: 254
H82: 128
PH: 66
AAHH: 218
NNBH: 97
CH: 172

"Go, Tell It on the Mountain"
found in:
UMH: 251
H82: 99
PH: 29
AAHH: 202
NNBH: 92
NCH: 154

CH: 167
LBW: 70

"Rise, Shine, You People"
found in:
UMH: 187
LBW: 393

"God of Grace and God of Glory"
found in:
UMH: 577
H82: 594/595
PH: 420
NCH: 436
CH: 464
LBW: 415

"I Want to Walk as a Child of the Light"
found in:
UMH: 206
H82: 490

"Arise, Shine"
found in:
CCB: 2
Renew: 123

"Shine, Jesus, Shine"
found in:
CCB: 81
Renew: 247

Prayer for the Day / Collect
O God who is the light than can never be extinguished: Grant
us the faith to come to your light in Jesus that we may know

the joy of your salvation and gladly proclaim you to all the world; through Jesus Christ our Savior. Amen.

OR

We have come into your presence, O God, because your light and love have drawn us here. We come as we are and offer ourselves to your saving grace. Open our eyes to see the truth of your light that we might live faithfully as disciples of Jesus Christ, your Son. Amen.

Prayer of Confession

Leader: Let us confess to God and before one another our sins and especially our preference for the shadows that hide us from God's truth.

People: We confess to you, O God, and before one another that we have sinned. You have sent your light into the world and though we say we follow Jesus, the light of the world, we know that often we prefer to hide in the shadows. We do not want others to know who we are. We don't want you to know who we are. We don't want to know who we are. In spite of all Jesus has taught us, we find it difficult to believe that you love us as we are. Forgive our lack of faith and help us to know of your love that we can joyfully share your love and grace with others. Amen.

Leader: God does love us as we are, even when we are people of little faith. Receive the light of God's love in your life and share that light with others.

Prayers of the People (and the Lord's Prayer)

We praise and glorify your name, O God, for your light that draws us to your beauty. Your light is eternal and chases away the darkness forever.

(The following paragraph may be used if a separate prayer of confession has not been used.)
We confess to you, O God, and before one another that we have sinned. You have sent your light into the world and though we say we follow Jesus, the light of the world, we know that often we prefer to hide in the shadows. We do not want others to know who we are. We don't want you to know who we are. We don't want to know who we are. In spite of all Jesus has taught us, we find it difficult to believe that you love us as we are. Forgive our lack of faith and help us to know of your love that we can joyfully share your love and grace with others.

We give you thanks for all the beauty of the world that light reveals to us. We thank you for the brilliance of the sun and for the reflective light of the moon. We thank you for those who have come into our lives and have shared your light with us. Most of all we thank you for Jesus who came as the light of the world so that we might find the true way to you.

(Other thanksgivings may be offered.)
We pray for those who dwell in darkness. We know we are one with them. We pray that as you continue to shine your loving light upon all your creatures, you would help us to reflect that light so that those around us may know of your loving kindness.

(Other intercessions may be offered.)
All these things we ask in the name of our Savior Jesus Christ who taught us to pray together saying:
Our Father... Amen.

(Or if the Our Father is not used at this point in the service)
All this we ask in the name of the Blessed and Holy Trinity. Amen.

Baptism of Our Lord / Epiphany 1 / Ordinary Time 1

Genesis 1:1-5
Acts 19:1-7
Mark 1:4-11

Call to Worship
Leader: Ascribe to the Lord glory and strength.
People: Ascribe to the Lord the glory due God's name.
Leader: The voice of God is full of majesty.
People: The voice of God flashes forth flames of fire.
Leader: May the Lord give us strength.
People: May the Lord bless us with peace!

OR

Leader: When God began to create, God said, "Let there be light."
People: And there was light, and it was good.
Leader: When Jesus came up from the waters of baptism,
People: the light and glory of God showed us his was the true light.
Leader: Let us worship the One who brings us light in nature and in the Christ.
People: All glory and praise to you, O God, and to your Christ.

Hymns and Sacred Songs
(As we continue the theme of light, many of last week's hymns may be helpful as well.)
"When Jesus Came to Jordan"
found in:

UMH: 252
PH: 72

"I Want to Walk as a Child of the Light"
found in:
UMH: 206
H82: 490

"Have Thine Own Way, Lord"
found in:
UMH: 382
AAHH: 449
NNBH: 206
CH: 588

"O Come and Dwell in Me"
found in:
UMH: 388

"Word of God, Come Down to Earth"
found in:
UMH: 182
H82: 633

"Of the Father's Love Begotten"
found in:
UMH: 184
H82: 82
PH: 309
NCH: 118
CH: 104
LBW: 42

"Rise, Shine, You People"
found in:

UMH: 187
LBW: 393

"Christ Is the World's Light"
found in:
UMH: 188
H82: 542

Prayer for the Day / Collect

O God who calls us your Beloved: Grant us the faith to trust in your love so that we may be loving as well as beloved; through Jesus Christ our Savior. Amen.

OR

We come to you, O God, for the words of life. Most of all we come to hear those wondrous words where you declare that we are your beloved children. Help us to believe in your love so that we may share your love with those around us. Amen.

Prayer of Confession

Leader: The light has come into the world and we have wandered off into our own darkness.

People: We confess that we are threatened by your light, O God. It shows us who we are and who we need to be. We do not like what we see. We are not the kind of people you created us to be. We do not love you with all of our being and we love ourselves ever so much more than we care about others. We see who we should be, and we know we would need to give up our petty jealousies and regard others as importantly as we regard ourselves. Forgive us for fleeing from your light and give us the courage to see ourselves clearly and still trust that you love us and will give us your Spirit to enable us to follow Jesus. Amen.

Leader: God is light and there is no darkness in God. The darkness cannot overcome the light even when the darkness is of our own choosing. God forgives us and empowers us. Thanks be to God.

Prayers of the People (and the Lord's Prayer)
We worship and praise your name, O God, for you are the One who created the light. When there was nothing but chaos and darkness, you spoke and the wonder of light came into being. You were not content to just give us natural light but you spoke the word and gave us the true light that is Christ.

(The following paragraph may be used if a separate prayer of confession has not been used.)
We confess that we are threatened by your light, O God. It shows us who we are and who we need to be. We do not like what we see. We are not the kind of people you created us to be. We do not love you with all of our being and we love ourselves ever so much more than we care about others. We see who we should be, and we know we would need to give up our petty jealousies and regard others as importantly as we regard ourselves. Forgive us for fleeing from your light and give us the courage to see ourselves clearly and still trust that you love us and will give us your Spirit to enable us to follow Jesus.

We give you thanks for all the ways your light has shone into our lives. You have blessed us with the beauty of your creation, which unfolds before us in majesty and splendor. You have given us insight that allows us to understand others and ourselves better. You have even opened yourself to us that we might know you and love you. When all else fails us, your light is eternal.

We offer up to the healing light of your presence the ills of this world. May those lost in the darkness of illness, poverty, violence, sin, grief, and lostness have their eyes opened to the glorious presence of your light and your salvation.

All this we ask in the name of Jesus who taught us to pray together, saying:

Our Father... Amen.

(Or if the Lord's Prayer is not used at this point in the service.)

This we ask in the name of the Blessed and Holy Trinity. Amen.

Epiphany 2 / Ordinary Time 2

1 Samuel 3:1-10 (11-20)
1 Corinthians 6:12-20
John 1:43-51

Call to Worship
Leader: God searches us and knows us.
People: God knows when we sit down and when we rise.
Leader: God knows the paths we choose
People: and is acquainted with all our ways.
Leader: God's thoughts are so vast.
People: We could count them forever without end.

OR

Leader: God has called some of us to be leaders.
People: May our leaders be blessed by God.
Leader: God has called some of us to follow.
People: May the followers do so with integrity.
Leader: All of us have been called to discern who is to lead.
People: Let us listen to God so that following or leading we may always be in God's path.

Hymns and Sacred Songs
"Guide Me, O Thou Great Jehovah"
found in:
UMH: 127
H82: 690
PH: 281
AAHH: 138/139/140
NNBH: 232
NCH: 18/19

CH: 622
LBW: 343

"Great Is Thy Faithfulness"
found in:
UMH: 140
PH: 276
AAHH: 158
NNBH: 45
NCH: 423
CH: 86

"If Thou but Suffer God to Guide Thee"
found in:
UMH: 142
H82: 635
PH: 282
NCH: 410
CH: 565
LBW: 453

"He Leadeth Me: O Blessed Thought"
found in:
UMH: 128
AAHH: 142
NNBH: 235
CH: 545
LBW: 501

"O God, Our Help in Ages Past"
found in:
UMH: 117
H82: 680
AAHH: 170
NNBH: 46

NCH: 25
CH: 67
LBW: 320

"The Lord's My Shepherd, I'll Not Want"
found in:
UMH: 136
PH: 170
CH: 78
LBW: 451

"The Lord's My Shepherd"
found in:
PH: 174

"The Lord's My Shepherd, All My Need"
found in:
PH: 175

"The Lord Is My Shepherd"
found in:
AAHH: 426
NNBH: 241

"The Lord My God My Shepherd Is"
found in:
H82: 663

"The King of Love My Shepherd Is"
found in:
UMH: 138
H82: 645/646
PH: 171
NCH: 248
LBW: 456

"Make Me a Captive, Lord"
found in:
UMH: 421
PH:378

"O Master, Let Me Walk with Thee"
found in:
UMH: 430
H82: 659/660
PH: 357
NNBH: 445
NCH: 503
CH: 602
LBW: 492

"Be Thou My Vision"
found in:
UMH: 451
H82: 488
PH: 339
NCH: 451
CH: 595

Prayer for the Day / Collect
O God who has always raised up leaders to guide your
people: Give us the wisdom to discern who you are calling to
lead us now so that we may be your faithful people; through
Jesus Christ our Savior. Amen.

OR

We come into your presence today, O God, knowing that
you are the true leader of your people. We know that you
also call human leaders to help us find your way. Whether

we are being called to lead or follow at this time, give us the wisdom to discern our role and your direction. Amen.

Prayer of Confession
Leader: Let us confess to God and before one another the ways in which we have failed to be faithful as leaders and followers in God's paths.
People: We confess to you, our God and our guide, that we don't like to follow. We resist even following you though we seldom admit it but we are even more resistant when your leadership means our following other human beings. We think we always know best and that we can always discern your way for us and your people as well as anyone. Forgive us for our pride and self-centeredness. Help us in all humility to accept our role, whether as follower or leader and to trust that you will always lead us deeper into your reign.
Leader: God comes to lead us to full salvation. Whenever we stray, God is there to help us get back on the right path. Knowing God's love and forgiveness, let us follow God in all we do.

Prayers of the People (and the Lord's Prayer)
We worship and adore you, O God, for you are the One who never leaves us or forsakes us. You are determined to bring salvation to all of your creation and willing to grant your people to be a part of that great work.

(The following paragraph may be used if a separate prayer of confession has not been used.)
We confess to you, our God and our guide, that we don't like to follow. We resist even following you though we seldom admit it but we are even more resistant when your leadership means our following other human beings. We think we always know best and that we can always discern your way

for us and your people as well as anyone. Forgive us for our pride and self-centeredness. Help us in all humility to accept our role, whether of follower or leader, and to trust that you will always lead us deeper into your reign.

We thank you for the faithfulness with which you have raised up leaders for your people. We thank you for the leaders who helped to found this congregation and for those who have faithfully served through the years. We thank you for those who serve you by serving us as our leaders now and for those you will raise up to lead us in the future.

(Other thanksgivings may be offered.)
We offer our prayers for our leaders. We know the task is not easy but that you are sufficient for all their needs. Bless them and us that we may all be faithful followers of our Good Shepherd.

(Other intercessions may be offered.)
All these things we ask in the name of our Savior Jesus Christ who taught us to pray together saying:
Our Father... Amen.

(Or if the Lord's Prayer is not used at this point in the service)
All this we ask in the name of the Blessed and Holy Trinity. Amen.

Epiphany 3 / Ordinary Time 3

Jonah 3:1-5, 10
1 Corinthians 7:29-31
Mark 1:14-20

Call to Worship
Leader: Who is it that you wait for?
People: It is for God alone that our souls wait.
Leader: Where does your hope come from?
People: Our hope is in our God.
Leader: Who will deliver you?
People: God, our rock and refuge, is our deliverer.

OR

Leader: "The time has come," Jesus says, "repent and believe."
People: We feel really bad about some of the things we have done.
Leader: That is a good thing, but Jesus calls us to repent, to change.
People: Do we really have to change to follow Jesus?
Leader: We need to change our lives and trust that his way is best.
People: It won't be easy. It may take us a while. But we will repent and trust in Jesus the Christ.

OR

Leader: God looks and sees that we are headed for destruction.
People: We also can see that our way will lead to death.

Leader: Jesus calls us to forsake our old ways and trust in him.
People: The ways of this world have not brought us life.
Leader: Repent, change, and trust in the way of Jesus.
People: We will change and trust in Jesus.

Hymns and Sacred Songs
"Come, Sinners, to the Gospel Feast"
found in:
UMH: 339

"*Tu Has Venido a la Orilla*" ("Lord, You Have Come to the Lakeshore")
found in:
UMH: 344
PH: 377
NCH: 173
CH: 342

"Spirit Song"
found in:
UMH: 347
AAHH: 321
CH: 352

"Turn Your Eyes Upon Jesus"
found in:
UMH: 349
NNBH: 195

"It's Me, It's Me, O Lord"
found in:
UMH: 352
NNBH: 496
CH: 579

"I Surrender All"
found in:
UMH: 354
AAHH: 396
NNBH: 198

"Dear Lord and Father of Mankind"
found in:
UMH: 358
H82: 652/653
PH: 345
NCH: 502
CH: 594
LBW: 506

Prayer for the Day / Collect
O God who created us for love and for life: Grant us the courage to forsake our ways of hatred and death that we might enter fully into your reign; through Jesus Christ our Savior. Amen.

OR

We hear today the call of Jesus to repent and believe. The work of change is never easy and seldom quick, but we trust that Jesus has the words of life and the way of salvation. Today we will come to Jesus. Amen.

Prayer of Confession
Leader: Jesus calls us this day to repent and believe. Let us confess that we have not yet fully embraced his call.
People: God of us all, we hear the call of Jesus to forsake our self-centered ways, our greed, our jealousy, our anger, and our violence. We hear him call us to give up power and take our place with him in service to the world.

We want to trust that his way is true but we worry that people will take advantage of us and we will look silly. We confess that we have very little taste for change. Forgive us for our foolishness and fear. Empower us with your Spirit that we may truly become, once again, disciples of our Savior Jesus. Amen.
Leader: God calls us because God loves us. Believe in God's love and grace and follow Jesus to life and joy.

Prayers of the People (and the Lord's Prayer)
Creator of life and all that is good and holy, we worship you and praise your holy name. You are wisdom, life, and joy eternal. We come to praise your name and worship you.

(The following paragraph may be used if a separate prayer of confession has not been used.)
God of us all, we hear the call of Jesus to forsake our self-centered ways, our greed, our jealousy, our anger, and our violence. We hear him call us to give up power and take our place with him in service to the world. We want to trust that his way is true but we worry that people will take advantage of us and we will look silly. We confess that we have very little taste for change. Forgive us for our foolishness and fear. Empower us with your Spirit that we may truly become, once again, disciples of our Savior Jesus.

We give you thanks for all the blessings you have brought to us. We especially give you thanks for giving us the word of life in Jesus the Christ. We thank you for his teachings in words and in actions. We know that all he said and did is a precious gift that shows us the way to life as you meant for us to live it.

(Other thanksgivings may be offered.)
We pray for ourselves this day because it is only by your power and grace that we are able to change the way we

live. We pray for those we have hurt because we have not followed the way of Jesus. We pray for those who have been hurt because we have allowed others to do harm in our name. We pray that we may be bold and follow Jesus so that the way of your reign may come to its completion.

(Other intercessions may be offered.)
All these things we ask in the name of our Savior Jesus Christ who taught us to pray together saying:
Our Father... Amen.

(Or if the Lord's Prayer is not used at this point in the service)
All this we ask in the name of the Blessed and Holy Trinity. Amen.

Epiphany 4 / Ordinary Time 4

Deuteronomy 18:15-20
1 Corinthians 8:1-13
Mark 1:21-28

Call to Worship
Leader: Praise the Lord!
People: We will give thanks to God with our whole hearts.
Leader: Full of honor and majesty is God's work.
People: God's righteousness endures forever.
Leader: To be in awe of God is the beginning of wisdom.
People: We will practice God's wisdom and praise God's name.

OR

Leader: God calls each of us to enter the kingdom.
People: We come today to say yes to God's invitation.
Leader: In God's reign we become a community.
People: We come today to accept our place in this sacred gathering.
Leader: In Christ, we are all united into his body.
People: We come to honor one another as we honor the Christ.

Hymns and Sacred Songs
"O for a Thousand Tongues to Sing"
found in:
UMH: 57
H82: 493
PH: 466
AAHH: 184

NNBH: 23
NCH: 42
CH: 5
LBW: 559

"All Creatures of Our God and King"
found in:
UMH: 62
H82: 400
PH: 455
AAHH: 147
NNBH: 33
NCH: 17
CH: 22
LBW: 527

"We, Thy People, Praise Thee"
found in:
UMH: 67

"The Church's One Foundation"
found in:
UMH: 545/546
H82: 525
PH: 442
AAHH: 337
NNBH: 297
NCH: 386
CH: 272
LBW: 369

"O Church of God, United"
found in:
UMH: 547

"Where Charity and Love Prevail"
found in:
UMH: 549
H82: 581
NCH: 396
LBW: 126

"Help Us Accept Each Other"
found in:
UMH: 560
PH: 358
NCH: 388
CH: 487

"We Are the Church"
found in:
UMH: 558

"We Are One"
found in:
AAHH: 323

"There Is One Lord"
found in:
Renew: 161

"I Am Loved"
found in:
CCB: 80

"They'll Know We Are Christians by Our Love"
found in:
CCB: 78

"Unity"
found in:
CCB: 59

Prayer for the Day / Collect

O God who knew that it was not good for a human to dwell alone: Grant us the wisdom to accept our place in your reign as we accept those you have invited in; through Jesus Christ our Savior whose body we are. Amen.

OR

We gather as your people today, God, knowing that we can never fully worship you or serve you alone. There is too much to do and too much to understand for anyone of us. Help us to embrace each other as sisters and brothers, as parts joined to us in Christ Jesus. Amen.

Prayer of Confession

Leader: God has called us to be people together. Let us together confess how we have failed to love one another.

People: We confess to you, O God, and before these, our sisters and brothers, that we have failed to live in unity as you created us to do. We have failed to acknowledge each other as brothers and sisters in your holy family, and we have sinned against our Savior as we have sinned against one another. We have not cried with those who weep; we have not danced with those who rejoice. We are more concerned about our own comfort and tastes in worship than in whether or not people get connected with you. We are more interested in our own salvation than whether or not others are rescued from the hell that binds them. Forgive us for our sins against each other and against you. By the power of your Spirit enable us to

74

see you in people we meet so that we may honor you as we serve them. Amen.

Leader: God is the great prodigal Father who offers love and grace without limits. As you accept each other know that God accepts you.

Prayers of the People (and the Lord's Prayer)

We worship and adore you, O God, because as our Creator you know us completely. You know that we cannot be fully human unless we unite ourselves with all humanity. You created us as the people of God so that together we might more fully understand you and together we might more fully serve you through serving one another.

(The following paragraph may be used if a separate prayer of confession has not been used.)

We confess to you, O God, and before these, our sisters and brothers, that we have failed to live in unity as you created us to do. We have failed to acknowledge each other as brothers and sisters in your holy family, and we have sinned against our Savior as we have sinned against one another. We have not cried with those who weep; we have not danced with those who rejoice. We are more concerned about our own comfort and tastes in worship than in whether or not people get connected with you. We are more interested in our own salvation than whether or not others are rescued from the hell that binds them. Forgive us for our sins against each other and against you. By the power of your Spirit enable us to see you in people we meet so that we may honor you as we serve them.

We give you thanks for our place in your church with all the saints. We thank you for those who teach us and who care for us. We thank you for those who irritate and annoy us. They are our brothers and sisters and they all belong to you. We thank you for those who have gifts and talents that we do not possess so that they may help us do your work here on earth.

(Other thanksgivings may be offered.)
We offer up to your loving grace all our church. We know that we cannot be whole as persons until we are whole as a community. Bind us together in your love until the entire world shall see you in our midst.

(Other intercessions may be offered.)
All these things we ask in the name of our Savior Jesus Christ who taught us to pray together saying:
Our Father... Amen.

(Or if the Our Father is not used at this point in the service)
All this we ask in the name of the Blessed and Holy Trinity. Amen.

Epiphany 5 / Ordinary Time 5

Isaiah 40:21-31
1 Corinthians 9:16-23
Mark 1:29-39

Call to Worship
Leader: Praise our God!
People: How good it is to sing praises to God!
Leader: God is gracious.
People: It is fitting to sing God's praises.
Leader: Sing to God with thanksgiving.
People: Make music to our God.

OR

Leader: We come together as disciples of Jesus.
People: We come to hear again the good news of God.
Leader: We have come to hear of God's graciousness toward us
People: so that we may go and tell others.
Leader: We come together as disciples of Jesus.
People: We leave as proclaimers of the gospel.

OR

Leader: We come to worship the One who created us.
People: God has created us in the divine image.
Leader: We cannot be our true selves
People: unless we spend time with our Creator.
Leader: We cannot be like God
People: if we do not open our hearts to God.

Hymns and Sacred Songs
Sent in Mission
"Jesus Calls Us"
found in:
UMH: 398
H82: 549/550
NNBH: 183
NCH: 171/172
CH: 337
LBW: 494

"Whom Shall I Send?"
found in:
UMH: 582

"O Zion, Haste"
found in:
UMH: 573
H82: 539
NNBH: 422
LBW: 397

"Go, Make of All Disciples"
found in:
UMH: 571

"We've a Story to Tell to the Nations"
found in:
UMH: 569
NNBH: 416
CH: 484

"*Sois la Semilla*" ("You Are the Seed")
found in:
UMH: 583

NCH: 528
CH: 478

"Lord, You Give the Great Commission"
found in:
UMH: 584
H82: 528
PH: 529
CH: 459

"How Shall They Hear the Word Of God"
found in:
UMH: 649

"Here I Am, Lord"
found in:
UMH: 593
PH: 525
AAHH: 567

"Pass It On"
found in:
UMH: 572
NNBH: 417
CH: 477

"We Are His Hands"
found in:
CCB: 85

"We Are the Light of the World"
found in:
Renew: 288

Prayer

"Near to the Heart of God"
found in:
UMH: 472
PH: 527
NNBH: 316
CH: 581

"Be Thou My Vision"
found in:
UMH: 451
H82: 488
PH: 339
NCH: 451
CH: 595

"Move Me"
found in:
UMH: 471

"Lead Me, Lord"
found in:
UMH: 473
AAHH: 145
CH: 593
NNBH: 341
Renew: 175

"As the Deer"
found in:
CCB: 83

"Fill My Cup, Lord"
found in:
CCB: 47

"Sanctuary"
found in:
CCB: 87

"Your Loving Kindness Is Better than Life"
found in:
CCB: 26

"Stay with Me"
found in:
Renew: 169

"Stay Here"
found in:
Renew: 170

Prayer for the Day / Collect
O God who created us in your own image: Grant us the wisdom to renew that image always by coming to know you more fully; through Jesus Christ our Lord. Amen.

OR

O God who sent Jesus to proclaim the good news of your grace to your children: Grant that we who have received your loving kindness may share the good news with those around us; through Jesus Christ our Lord. Amen.

OR

You created us in your image, God, and have invited us to live in your presence. You have included us as part of your holy family and you call us to invite others to join us. Help us to find our joy in being with you and telling others of your loving kindness. Amen.

Prayer of Confession

Leader: Let us confess our sins to God and before one another.

People: We confess to you, O God, and before our sisters and brothers that we have failed in bearing your image clearly in both our speech and our actions. We have not drawn close to you and learned to know you as you have desired. We have failed to share the good news of your loving kindness with those who need to hear it most. Forgive us our failures and by the power of your Spirit draw us close to you and send us out to share with others. Amen.

Leader: God does love us and is always willing to forgive us and gather us into the arms of divine love. Draw close to God with confidence and share God's love with abandon.

Prayers of the People (and the Lord's Prayer)

We worship and adore you, Creator of all, for you are worthy of praises we are not able to express. You created us in your own image and come to share your life with us day by day.

(The following paragraph may be used if a separate prayer of confession has not been used.)

We confess to you, O God, and before our sisters and brothers that we have failed in bearing your image clearly in both our speech and our actions. We have not drawn close to you and learned to know you as you have desired. We have failed to share the good news of your loving kindness with those who need to hear it most. Forgive us our failures and by the power of your Spirit draw us close to you and send us out to share with others. Amen.

We give you thanks for all the ways you have expressed your love to us. We thank you for your presence both unmediated and shared through others.

(Other thanksgivings may be offered.)
We offer up to you those who have not yet learned of your great love for them. We offer up ourselves that we might be so filled with the power of your Spirit that we will share you through each word we speak and each action we take.

(Other intercessions may be offered.)
All these things we ask in the name of our Savior Jesus Christ who taught us to pray together saying:
Our Father... Amen.

(Or if the Lord's Prayer is not used at this point in the service)
All this we ask in the name of the Blessed and Holy Trinity. Amen.

Epiphany 6 / Ordinary Time 6

2 Kings 5:1-14
1 Corinthians 9:24-27
Mark 1:40-45

Call to Worship
Leader: Let us extol our God,
People: for God has drawn us up.
Leader: We have cried to God,
People: and God has healed us.
Leader: Weeping may linger for the night,
People: but joy comes in the morning.

OR

Leader: Let us come before our God, our healer.
People: We come in our brokenness and sin.
Leader: God invites us to open up the wounds we carry.
People: We know that God wants to heal our hurts.
Leader: Let us trust the One who loves us more than we can know.
People: We offer our hurts and ask for God's healing.

Hymns and Sacred Songs
"I'll Praise My Maker While I've Breath"
found in:
UMH: 60
H82: 42
PH: 253
CH: 20

"Maker, in Whom We Live"
found in:
UMH: 88

"For the Beauty of the Earth"
found in:
UMH: 92
H82: 416
PH: 473
NNBH: 8
NCH: 28
CH: 56
LBW: 561

"There Is a Balm in Gilead"
found in:
UMH: 375
H82: 676
PH: 394
AAHH: 524
NNBH: 489
NCH: 553
CH: 501

"It Is Well with My Soul"
found in:
UMH: 377
AAHH: 377
NNBH: 255
CH: 561

"Amazing Grace"
found in:
UMH: 378
H82: 671

PH: 280
AAHH: 271/272
NNBH: 161/163
NCH: 547/548
CH: 546
LBW: 448

"He Touched Me"
found in:
UMH: 367
AAHH: 373
NNBH: 147
CH: 564

"Because He Lives"
found in:
UMH: 364
AAHH: 281
NNBH: 120
CH: 562

"*Pues Si Vivimos*" ("When We Are Living")
found in:
UMH: 356
PH: 400
NCH: 499
CH: 536

Prayer for the Day / Collect
O God, who created all to be good and whole: Grant us
faith that we may trust our hurts and wounds to you and
find ourselves made whole through Jesus Christ our Savior.
Amen.

OR

We come to worship the God who created all things good. Creation has strayed from God's good intentions and there are many wounds and scars on all. We, too, have suffered our hurts. We come in faith to offer all creation and ourselves to God's healing touch. Amen.

Prayer of Confession

Leader: Let us confess the ways in which we have been wounded and the ways we have wounded others.

People: We confess to you, O God our healer, that we have been part of the wounding of your creation. We have not properly cared for the earth, air, and water you provide for us. We have not properly cared for the plants and animals that you committed to our care. We have not properly cared for our brothers and sisters whom you created In your own image and filled with your own life breath. We have not even properly cared for ourselves. We have abused our bodies and ignored our spiritual needs. Forgive us and lead us into your healing for ourselves and make us your healers for all creation. Amen.

Leader: God desires to heal all that is created. God especially desires to heal those made in God's own image. Know that God offers you forgiveness and healing and the Holy Spirit to make you part of God's healing work.

Prayers of the People (and the Lord's Prayer)

We worship and adore you, our Creator and our healer. You made all things good and have offered all creation for our needs and for our care.

(The following paragraph may be used if a separate prayer of confession has not been used.)

We confess to you, O God our healer, that we have been part

of the wounding of your creation. We have not properly cared for the earth, air, and water you provide for us. We have not properly cared for the plants and animals that you committed to our care. We have not properly cared for our brothers and sisters whom you created in your own image and filled with your own life breath. We have not even properly cared for ourselves. We have abused our bodies and ignored our spiritual needs. Forgive us and lead us into your healing for ourselves and make us your healers for all creation.

You have given many parts of creation an ability to heal the wounds we inflict on each other and ourselves. You have created us to be your healers. You have made us in your image and filled us with your life breath so that we may be part of your work of healing.

(Other thanksgivings may be offered.)
We offer up to you all the hurts and wounds of creation. We offer you the earth that you created so well and we have all but destroyed. We offer to you the memory of those animals and plants that you called good and we wiped from existence. We offer to you our sisters and brothers who are broken and in need of healing: those in poverty, pain, and involved in violence; those who are hungry in body, mind, or spirit; those who are lonely, rejected, and do not know your love.

(Other intercessions may be offered.)
All these things we ask in the name of our Savior Jesus Christ who taught us to pray together saying:
Our Father... Amen.

(Or if the Lord's Prayer is not used at this point in the service)
All this we ask in the name of the blessed and Holy Trinity. Amen.

Transfiguration of Our Lord
(Last Sunday after Epiphany)

2 Kings 2:1-12
2 Corinthians 4:3-6
Mark 9:2-9

Call to Worship

Leader: God, the Mighty One, speaks and summons the earth,

People: from the rising of the sun to its setting.

Leader: Out of Zion God shines forth.

People: Our God comes and does not keep silence.

Leader: God gathers the faithful ones.

People: Even the heavens declare God's righteousness.

OR

Leader: Come to the light and let God heal you.

People: We come in our blindness to God's work.

Leader: Come to the light and let God heal you.

People: We look and we do not see.

Leader: Come to the light and let God heal you.

People: God's light has filled us and now we see.

OR

Leader: Come to the mountain and see the truth.

People: We come as disciples of old.

Leader: See Jesus again and know him anew.

People: We want to know Jesus the Christ.

Leader: Jesus comes among us to be revealed.

People: We worship him so that we might follow him.

Hymns and Sacred Songs
"Open My Eyes, that I May See"
found in:
UMH: 454
PH: 324
NNBH: 219
CH: 586

"Be Thou My Vision"
found in:
UMH: 451
H82: 488
PH: 339
NCH: 451
CH: 595

"Seek the Lord"
found in:
UMH: 124

"Give to the Winds Thy Fears"
found in:
UMH: 129
PH: 286
NCH: 404

"Behold a Broken World"
found in:
UMH: 426

"God of Grace and God of Glory"
found in:
UMH: 577
H82: 594/595

PH: 420
NCH: 436
CH: 464
LWB: 415

"God of Love and God of Power"
found in:
UMH: 578

"O Spirit of the Living God"
found in:
UMH: 539
H82: 531
NCH: 263
LBW: 388

"Open Our Eyes, Lord"
found in:
CCB: 77

"Something Beautiful"
found in:
CCB: 84

"Refiner's Fire"
found in:
CCB: 79

Prayer for the Day / Collect
O God who created light and called it good: Grant us new
eyes to see the reality of your presence among us; through
Jesus Christ our Savior. Amen.

OR

You have made us with eyes to see and with ears to hear, God our Creator. Help us to see not only the beauty of creation but also the reality of your presence here among us in all that is happening in our world. Amen.

OR

O God who transfigured Jesus and transformed the disciples upon the mount: Grant that we may also be transformed anew as we behold the Christ among us; through Jesus Christ our Savior. Amen.

Prayer of Confession
Leader: Let us confess our sins and our blindness to our God and before one another.
People: We confess to you, O God, and before one another that we live in darkness and that is of our own will. You have come and offered us light and vision that sees reality as you see it, but we prefer the lies of the world. We prefer to see things from our own perspective and our own importance. Forgive us our willful foolishness and by the power of your Spirit fill us with light anew. Amen.
Leader: God is light and in God there is no darkness at all. God sends forth the light to fill you and give you life. In the name of the Christ, know you are forgiven.

Prayers of the People (and the Lord's Prayer)
We worship and adore you, O God of light, for in you there is nothing dark. Your wisdom, power, and love are not limited. You speak and the darkness and chaos flee from your light.

(The following paragraph may be used if a separate prayer of confession has not been used.)

We confess to you, O God, and before one another that we live in darkness and that of our own will. You have come and offered us light and vision that sees reality as you see it, but we prefer the lies of the world. We prefer to see things from our own perspective and our own importance. Forgive us our willful foolishness and by the power of your Spirit fill us with light anew.

We give thanks for all the ways your light has shone in our lives. In the lives of parents, teachers, preachers, and friends, you have shown to us the way. You have opened our eyes and let us see the reality of love and grace that is you.

(Other thanksgivings may be offered.)

We pray for all who live in the darkness and desperately need your light to show them the way. We understand their confusion because we have been there and sometimes find ourselves there again. As you bring your gracious light into their lives, show us how we can be part of the ministry of light with our Savior Jesus.

(Other intercessions may be offered.)

All these things we ask in the name of our Savior Jesus Christ who taught us to pray together saying:
Our Father... Amen.

(Or if the Lord's Prayer is not used at this point in the service)

All this we ask in the name of the Blessed and Holy Trinity. Amen.

Ash Wednesday

Joel 2:1-2, 12-17 or Isaiah 58:1-12
2 Corinthians 5:20b—6:10
Matthew 6:1-6, 16-21

Call to Worship
Leader: Have mercy on us, O God, according to your stead-fast love;
People: according to your abundant mercy blot out our transgressions.
Leader: Wash us thoroughly from our iniquity,
People: and cleanse us from our sin.
Leader: Open our lips, O God,
People: and our mouths will declare your praise.

OR

Leader: Come before God your Creator and Judge.
People: We are unclean and not fit to face God.
Leader: God knows who you are! Come before God.
People: We come with trembling knowing our sinful selves.
Leader: God calls you to repent, to turn from death and embrace life.
People: God is gracious. We will turn from our sinful ways that lead us to death and embrace the life eternal.

Hymns and Sacred Songs
"Lord, Who Throughout These Forty Days"
found in:
UMH: 269
H82: 142
PH: 81

NCH: 211
CH: 180

"Come, Ye Sinners, Poor and Needy"
found in:
UMH: 340
Renew: 141

"Spirit Song"
found in:
UMH: 347
AAHH: 321
CH: 352
CCB: 51
Renew: 248

"It's Me, It's Me, O Lord"
found in:
UMH: 352
NNBH: 496
CH: 579

"I Surrender All"
found in:
UMH: 354
AAHH: 396
NNBH: 198

"*Pues Si Vivimos*" ("When We Are Living")
found in:
UMH: 356
PH: 400
NCH: 499
CH: 536

"Abide With Me"
found in:
UMH: 700
H82: 662
PH: 543
AAHH: 459
NNBH: 247
NCH: 99
CH: 636
LBW: 272

"Dear Lord and Father of Mankind"
found in:
UMH: 358
H82: 652/653
PH: 345
NCH: 502
CH: 594
LBW: 506

"Change My Heart, O God"
found in:
CCB: 56
Renew: 143

"Create in Me a Clean Heart"
found in:
CCB: 54
Renew: 181

Prayer for the Day / Collect
O God who calls us from death into life: Grant us the grace
to embrace our mortality that we may be filled with your
eternal life; through Jesus Christ our Savior. Amen.

OR

We come to worship you, O God, and to acknowledge that we are but sinful mortals. Our way leads to death and we have come to repent and return to you that we might have eternal life. Amen.

Prayer of Confession

Leader: Let us confess to God and before one another our sins and especially the ways we refuse to acknowledge our mortality and our sinfulness.

People: We confess to you, O God, and before one another that we have sinned. We live in a fantasy world acting as if we will live forever. We think we will always have time to amend our lives and turn to you. We deceive ourselves by saying, "We are not so bad. We are better than most." We forget that we are but dust. We forget that our sinfulness is great. Forgive us and help us to make amendment of our lives now that we may flee death and return to your life. Amen.

Leader: God desires our life and not our death. God graciously calls us and more graciously receives us into eternal life in Christ.

Prayers of the People (and the Lord's Prayer)

We worship and praise your name, O God, for you are the source of all goodness and of all life. It is in you alone that creation exists.

(The following paragraph may be used if a separate prayer of confession has not been used.)

We confess to you, O God, and before one another that we have sinned. We live in a fantasy world acting as if we will live forever. We think we will always have time to amend our lives and turn to you. We deceive ourselves by saying,

"We are not so bad. We are better than most." We forget that we are but dust. We forget that our sinfulness is great. Forgive us and help us to make amendment of our lives now that we may flee death and return to your life.

We give you thanks for our lives and your love that calls us to grow deeper in your love and life. We thank you for your Spirit that breathes into us eternal life in the midst of death. We thank you for Jesus who shows us the way to live in the joy of your life.

(Other thanksgivings may be offered.)
We pray for one another in our need and especially for those who are facing death without hope. For some it is physical death and for others it may be spiritual, emotional, or relational death. Send the gentle wind of your Spirit into their lives and help them to find in you the meaning of true life so that in life or death they will know your eternal life.

(Other intercessions may be offered.)
All these things we ask in the name of our Savior Jesus Christ who taught us to pray together saying:
Our Father... Amen.

(Or if the Our Father is not used at this point in the service)
All this we ask in the name of the Blessed and Holy Trinity. Amen.

Lent 1

Genesis 9:8-17
1 Peter 3:18-22
Mark 1:9-15

Call to Worship
Leader: To you, O God, we lift up our souls.
People: O God, in you we trust.
Leader: Make us to know your ways,
People: and teach us your paths.
Leader: Do not remember the sins of our youth.
People: Do not remember our transgressions.
Leader: Be mindful of your mercy, O God.
People: Hold us in your loving kindness.

OR

Leader: God calls us to eternal life, here and now.
People: The ways of God are peace and joy.
Leader: The ways of God are not our ways.
People: We are tempted to follow our own lead.
Leader: God is faithful and calls us to life.
People: We shall resist temptation and follow God.

OR

Leader: Jesus was the Son of God,
People: and he knew temptation.
Leader: We are children of God,
People: and we too know temptation.
Leader: In the very presence of temptation
People: we find the presence of God.

Hymns and Sacred Songs
"I Want a Principle Within"
found in:
UMH: 410

"Dear Lord and Father of Mankind"
found in:
UMH: 358
H82: 652/653
PH: 345
NCH: 502
CH: 594
LBW: 506

"This Is a Day of New Beginnings"
found in:
UMH: 383
CH: 518

"Take My Life, and Let It Be"
found in:
UMH: 399
H82: 707
PH: 391
NNBH: 213
NCH: 448
CH: 609
LBW: 406

"Lord, I Want to Be a Christian"
found in:
UMH: 402
PH: 372
AAHH: 463
NNBH: 156

NCH: 454
CH: 589

"Dear Lord, Lead Me Day by Day"
found in:
UMH: 411

"I Want to Walk as a Child of the Light"
found in:
UMH: 206
H82: 490

"Change My Heart, O God"
found in:
CCB: 56

"Refiner's Fire"
found in:
CCB: 79

Prayer for the Day / Collect

O God who created all life and called it good: Grant us the grace to find in following your path the true meaning of eternal life; through Jesus Christ our Savior. Amen.

OR

God, in Jesus you have shown us how to live as your children. You have shown us a life centered on you and on other people. You have shown us that it will involve temptation but that overcoming temptation is joy unspeakable and full of glory. Amen.

Prayer of Confession

Leader: Let us confess to God and before one another our

sins, including the sin of seeking forgiveness without seeking discipleship.

People: We confess to you, our Creator and Redeemer, and before our sisters and brothers that we are a people prone to sin. We are easily led astray as we follow our own folly rather than your wisdom. We want life everlasting, but we are less sure if we want eternal life here and now. We fear that it will mean a change in our lifestyle and the making of hard choices. Forgive us, and by the power of your Spirit help us to look to Jesus, the founder and forerunner of our faith that we may follow him in living fully unto you and for others, resisting the temptation to take a less blessed path. Amen.

Leader: God desires nothing more than to give his children life eternal, joyful, and abundant. Know that the grace of God is endless and sure and that God will guide you if you will follow.

Prayers of the People (and the Lord's Prayer)

We worship and adore you, O God of steadfast love, for you seek always to bring us to life in you. You know our frame and our wayward thinking ways and yet you come to lead us to a life that is blessed here and hereafter.

(The following paragraph may be used if a separate prayer of confession has not been used.)

We confess to you, our Creator and Redeemer, and before our sisters and brothers that we are a people prone to sin. We are easily led astray as we follow our own folly rather than your wisdom. We want life everlasting, but we are less sure if we want eternal life here and now. We fear that it will mean a change in our lifestyle and the making of hard choices. Forgive us, and by the power of your Spirit help us to look to Jesus, the founder and forerunner of our faith, that we may follow him in living fully unto you and for others, resisting the temptation to take a less blessed path.

We give you thanks for our Savior Jesus, who shows us the way to live in this life so that we are living in you. He knew that to follow the path of righteousness and holiness, he would be tempted. Yet he faced the tempter and stayed true to you. We thank you for your aid in helping us to follow his example.

(Other thanksgivings may be offered.)
We offer up to your care those of us who have been deluded by the tempter to seek salvation in paths other than your own. We have walked them enough to know that they do not satisfy and they do not bring life. Help us to not only be faithful followers of Jesus but also to invite others to join the journey with us.

(Other intercessions may be offered.)
All these things we ask in the name of our Savior Jesus Christ who taught us to pray together saying:
Our Father... Amen.

(Or if the Lord's Prayer is not used at this point in the service)
All this we ask in the name of the Blessed and Holy Trinity. Amen.

Lent 2

Genesis 17:1-7, 15-16
Romans 4:13-25
Mark 8:31-38

Call to Worship
Leader: Let all who are in awe of God offer praises!
People: In awe of our God we glorify the Almighty.
Leader: All the ends of the earth shall remember our God.
People: All nations shall turn to the Creator.
Leader: Future generations shall hear of our God.
People: God's deliverance will be told to those yet unborn.

OR

Leader: We come to praise our God and Creator.
People: How can we sing praises in these times?
Leader: Remember the days of old when God brought salvation.
People: We know that God has saved in the past.
Leader: Believe that God will once again bring salvation.
People: We praise the God who continues to bring life from death.

OR

Leader: We have come to celebrate our Savior, Jesus.
People: He came as God's Son to bring salvation.
Leader: Yet his life was not easy and death seemed to swallow him up.

People: But his suffering was for us and life came through him.

Leader: We are called to pick up our cross and follow him,

People: though it be through suffering our path leads to eternal life.

Hymns and Sacred Songs

"God of the Sparrow, God of the Whale"
found in:
UMH: 122
PH: 272
NCH: 32
CH: 70

"All My Hope Is Firmly Grounded"
found in:
UMH: 132
H82: 665
NCH: 408
CH: 88

"All My Help Comes from the Lord"
found in:
AAHH: 370

"Great Is Thy Faithfulness"
found in:
UMH: 140
PH: 276
AAHH: 158
NNBH: 45
NCH: 423
CH: 86

"Praise to the Lord, the Almighty"
found in:
UMH: 139
H82: 390
AAHH: 117
NNBH: 2
NCH: 22
CH: 25
LBW:543

"Precious Name"
found in:
UMH: 536
NNBH: 410
CH: 625

"Saranam, Saranam"
found in:
UMH: 523

"Leave It There"
found in:
UMH: 522
AAHH: 420
NNBH: 187

"Lift Every Voice and Sing"
found in:
UMH: 519
H82: 599
PH: 563
NNBH: 457
NCH: 593
CH: 631
LBW: 562

"O Thou, in Whose Presence"
found in:
UMH: 518
AAHH: 422

"Out of the Depths I Cry to You"
found in:
UMH: 515
H82: 666
PH: 240
NNBH: 207
NCH: 483
CH: 510
LBW: 295

"Come, Ye Disconsolate"
found in:
UMH: 510
AAHH: 421
NNBH: 264
CH: 502

Prayer for the Day / Collect

O God who created out of love and a desire for community: Grant us the insight to see that even in the worst of circumstances you are calling us and all creation to wholeness and salvation; through Jesus Christ our Savior. Amen.

OR

When we find ourselves in hard places because of our stand for Jesus, help us to remember that our suffering can be salvation for ourselves and for others when we offer it to you. Amen.

OR

Help us, O God, to remember the ways in which you have brought salvation to your people in ages past and in our own lives that we may find courage and hope in these days of trial. Amen.

Prayer of Confession

Leader: Let us confess to God and before one another the ways in which we have failed to be God's faithful people and, especially, where we have failed to trust in God.

People: We confess to you, faithful God, that we have not been your faithful people. We have not trusted you with our whole hearts or with our whole lives. We have looked too often at the circumstances around us and doubted your care. When taking our stand as disciples of Jesus would bring us ridicule or hardship, we have looked for an easy way out. Forgive us and send your Spirit upon us that we may amend our lives and live, once again, as your faithful children. Amen.

Leader: The God who created you out of love grants you forgiveness and invites you to live anew a life of faithfulness and discipleship.

Prayers of the People (and the Lord's Prayer)

We have come to this place to worship and adore you, O God who loves us eternally. In creation you gave us all we need to not only survive but to thrive and grow into the fullness of your likeness.

(The following paragraph may be used if a separate prayer of confession has not been used.)

We confess to you, faithful God, that we have not been your faithful people. We have not trusted you with our whole hearts or with our whole lives. We have looked too often at the circumstances around us and doubted your care. When taking our stand as disciples of Jesus would bring us ridicule or hardship, we have looked for an easy way out. Forgive us and send your Spirit upon us that we may amend our lives and live, once again, as your faithful children. Amen.

We give you thanks for your faithfulness in those times when we see revealed all around us and for those times when our eyes are unable to perceive what you are doing for us. We give you thanks for you gracious invitation to live as your children and as disciples of your Son, Jesus the Christ.

(Other thanksgivings may be offered.)
We offer our prayers of love and care for those who find themselves in trouble and distress for the lifestyle you have called them to follow. Grant them strength and faith so that they may experience the hope they have in you.

(Other intercessions may be offered.)
All these things we ask in the name of our Savior Jesus Christ who taught us to pray together saying:
Our Father... Amen.

(Or if the Lord's Prayer is not used at this point in the service)
All this we ask in the name of the Blessed and Holy Trinity. Amen.

Lent 3

Exodus 20:1-17
1 Corinthians 1:18-25
John 2:13-22

Call to Worship
Leader: The heavens are telling the glory of God,
People: the firmament proclaims God's handiwork.
Leader: Day to day pours forth speech,
People: and night to night declares knowledge.
Leader: The law of God is perfect.
People: It revives our souls.
Leader: God's ways are more desirable than fine gold.
Leader: They are more desirable than honey from the honeycomb.

OR

Leader: Come and heed the signs that God is showing us.
People: There are so many different signs out there.
Leader: How will you tell which are of God?
People: We will look for the work of God in them.
Leader: What will be the sign of God's activity?
People: We will find God at work wherever we find the cross.

OR

Leader: Come and learn the wisdom of our God.
People: God's ways seem so strange and, well, foolish.
Leader: What seems right and intelligent to you?
People: Human thought seems very smart.

Leader: How has following human thought worked out for you?
People: Perhaps it is time for us to try God's foolishness.

Hymns and Sacred Songs
"Immortal, Invisible, God Only Wise"
found in:
UMH: 103
H82: 423
PH: 263
NCH: 1
CH: 66
LBW: 526

"God of Many Names"
found in:
UMH: 105
CH: 452

"Creating God, Your Fingers Trace"
found in:
UMH: 109
PH: 134
NCH: 462
CH: 335
LBW: 527

"All Creatures of Our God and King"
found in:
UMH: 62
H82: 394/395
PH: 455
AAHH: 147
NNBH: 33

NCH: 117
CH: 22

"We, Thy People, Praise Thee"
found in:
UMH: 67

"How Great Thou Art"
found in:
UMH: 77
PH: 467
AAHH: 148
NNBH: 43
CH: 33
LBW: 532

"Hail, Thou Once Despised Jesus"
found in:
UMH: 325
H82: 495

"What Wondrous Love Is This"
found in:
UMH: 292
H82: 439
PH: 85
NCH: 223
CH: 200
LBW: 385

"In the Cross of Christ I Glory"
found in:
UMH: 295
H82: 441/442
PH: 84

NNBH: 104
NCH: 193/194
CH: 207
LBW: 104

"When I Survey the Wondrous Cross"
found in:
UMH: 298/299
H82: 474
PH: 100/101
AAHH: 243
NNBH: 113
NCH: 224
CH: 195
LBW: 482

"Holy Ground"
found in:
CCB: 5

"Awesome God"
found in:
CCB: 17

"You Arc"
found in:
CCB: 23

"Your Loving Kindness Is Better than Life"
found in:
CCB: 26

Prayer for the Day / Collect
O God who gives signs and wonders in the most common
things: Grant us the wisdom and vision to see where you are

calling us in the events of these days; through Jesus Christ our Savior. Amen.

OR

O God whose ways are far beyond our ways and whose thoughts are far beyond our thoughts: Grant us the wisdom to follow your wise ways even when they look foolish to us; through Jesus Christ our Savior. Amen.

OR

We come to worship you today, God, because you are the font of all wisdom and knowledge. We come as people easily seduced by the foolishness of the world. Help us to listen to you today so that we hear your words of wisdom and counsel. Amen.

Prayer of Confession
Leader: Let us confess to God and before one another our sins and especially how we allow the world to deceive us with its foolishness.
People: We confess to you, God, and before our sisters and brothers our sins, both in what we have done and in what we have failed to do. We confess that we have fallen to the allure of the world's foolishness. We have listened to those who say the goal of life is to amass wealth. We have listened to those who say that power and violence are the way to peace. We have listened to those who say we can only get ahead by climbing on the backs of others. Forgive us, good Lord, and empower us with your Spirit that we might hear once again your words of wisdom and guidance that we might live into life eternal. Amen.
Leader: God's wisdom is to always call back his faithless people and give them a new start. Know that God loves you,

forgives you, and sends you out wiser than when you came here if you have listened to God's voice.

Prayers of the People (and the Lord's Prayer)
We come to worship you because you are the Creator of all that is and is not. Your wisdom is deeper than any ocean and higher than any mountain. We cannot speak of it properly because we cannot comprehend it. It is your wisdom that caused all creation to come into being.

(The following paragraph may be used if a separate prayer of confession has not been used.)
We confess to you, God, and before our sisters and brothers our sins, both in what we have done and in what we have failed to do. We confess that we have fallen to the allure of the world's foolishness. We have listened to those who say the goal of life is to amass wealth. We have listened to those who say that power and violence are the way to peace. We have listened to those who say we can only get ahead by climbing on the backs of others. Forgive us, good Lord, and empower us with your Spirit that we might hear once again your words of wisdom and guidance that we might live into life eternal. Amen.

We give you thanks for all the blessings we have received from you and especially for the gift of your wisdom that directs our lives. You have spoken to us in prophets and seers, in psalmists and gospelers, in scientists and visionaries. You have written your love and law in the groundwork of creation.

(Other thanksgivings may be offered.)
We pray for those who have not yet discovered the wisdom of your ways, O God. We pray that as you offer them signs to point them to a life full and abundant in you, we may also be a sign of your love for them.

(Other intercessions may be offered.)
All these things we ask in the name of our Savior Jesus Christ
who taught us to pray together saying:
Our Father... Amen.

*(Or if the Lord's Prayer is not used at this point in the
service)*
All this we ask in the name of the Blessed and Holy Trinity.
Amen.

Lent 4

Numbers 21:4-9
Ephesians 2:1-10
John 3:14-21

Call to Worship
Leader: Give thanks to our good God!
People: We lift our voices in thanksgiving and praise.
Leader: God is the One who has redeemed us
People: and brought us together from many places.
Leader: To God let us offer our thanksgiving;
People: let us offer God our songs of joy.

OR

Leader: God calls us to the light.
People: If we come to the light, God will know who we are.
Leader: God already knows who we are.
People: Then our sisters and brothers will know.
Leader: They probably know more than you think.
People: Then we will know who we are and have to change.
Leader: That is God's plan to transform you into light.
People: We come to God's light in our hopes and in our fears.

Hymns and Sacred Songs
"Immortal, Invisible, God Only Wise"
found in:
UMH: 103

"When Morning Gilds the Skies"
found in:
UMH: 185

"Morning Has Broken"
found in:
UMH: 145

"All Things Bright and Beautiful"
found in:
UMH: 147

"Christ, Whose Glory Fills the Skies"
found in:
UMH: 173

"I Want to Walk as a Child of the Light"
found in:
UMH: 206

"Rise, Shine, You People"
found in:
UMH: 187

"Christ Is the World's Light"
found in:
UMH: 188

"Let There Be Light"
found in:
UMH: 440

"This Little Light of Mine"
found in:
UMH: 585

"Arise, Shine"
found in:
CCB: 2

"From the Rising of the Sun"
found in:
CCB: 4

"Open Our Eyes, Lord"
found in:
CCB: 77

"Shine, Jesus, Shine"
found in:
CCB: 81

Prayer for the Day / Collect

O God who dwells in eternal light: Grant us the wisdom and the courage to allow your light to flood our lives and cleanse us for service in your eternal reign; through Jesus Christ our Savior. Amen.

OR

We come to worship the God of light and grace. We come knowing we are people of darkness. We would rather point out the darkness in others than to acknowledge our own evil. As you come among us, help us to open ourselves to you and your cleansing light. Amen.

Prayer of Confession

Leader: Let us confess to God and before one another the sinful nature of our lives especially our choice of darkness rather than light.

People: We confess to you, our God and our Savior that we have sinned in the things we have done and left undone, the things we have said and left unsaid. We are especially aware this day of our desire for darkness rather than light. We know that we are not the people you created us to be, but we would rather stay that way, hoping the darkness will hide the truth — if not from you, at least from our brothers and sisters. But we confess not only to you but also to our sisters and brothers in Christ that we are not what we should be nor what we often appear to be. We are selfish, self-centered, and sometimes cruel in our treatment of others. We ask for God's forgiveness and for the forgiveness of our community of faith so that we might together seek God's light for ourselves and for our community. Amen.

Leader: God is the God of light, love, and grace. God desires our well-being and so sends grace and forgiveness and the opportunity to amend our lives. In the name of Christ Jesus, we are forgiven.

Prayers of the People (and the Lord's Prayer)
God of light and truth, we have come to adore you and offer our worship and praise to you. You are light and in you there is no darkness at all. Though we try to hide in the darkness around us, you see us and know us.

(The following paragraph may be used if a separate prayer of confession has not been used.)
We confess to you, our God and our Savior that we have sinned in the things we have done and left undone, the things we have said and left unsaid. We are especially aware this day of our desire for darkness rather than light. We know that we are not the people you created us to be, but we would rather stay that way, hoping the darkness will hide the truth — if not from you, at least from our brothers and sisters. But

we confess not only to you but also to our sisters and brothers in Christ that we are not what we should be nor what we often appear to be. We are selfish, self-centered, and sometimes cruel in our treatment of others. We ask for God's forgiveness and for the forgiveness of our community of faith so that we might together seek God's light for ourselves and for our community.

We give you thanks for the light that enables us to see the beauty of creation. We are awed at the wonders that have been created for our needs and for our delight. Most of all we give you thanks for Jesus, the light of the world, who comes to draw us to you and your light.

(Other thanksgivings may be offered.)
We offer up to you those who dwell in darkness: the darkness of poverty, hunger, violence, and want; the darkness of anger, revenge, and broken relationships; the darkness of evil that blinds and misdirects. May the glory of your light shine more brightly and may we, your people, reflect your light more clearly to those around us.

(Other intercessions may be offered.)
All these things we ask in the name of our Savior Jesus Christ who taught us to pray together saying:
Our Father... Amen.

(Or if the Lord's Prayer is not used at this point in the service)
All this we ask in the name of the Blessed and Holy Trinity. Amen.

Lent 5

Jeremiah 31:31-34
Hebrews 5:5-10
John 12:20-33

Call to Worship
Leader: Have mercy on us, O God, according to your stead-fast love.
People: Blot out our transgressions according to your abundant mercy.
Leader: We know our transgressions.
People: Our sins are ever before us.
Leader: Create in us a clean heart.
People: Put a new and right spirit within us.

OR

Leader: God calls us into covenant.
People: We come to join together with God.
Leader: Our covenant with God puts us in covenant with all God's children.
People: We are joined to one another as sisters and brothers.
Leader: Let us worship our God and serve our neighbors.
People: This is what it means to be God's people.

OR

Leader: God calls us to offer our worship and praise.
People: We are not worthy to worship God.
Leader: God calls us not because we are worthy but because God desires our worship and praise.

People: With joy we answer God's gracious invitation to worship.

Leader: Let us offer not only our praise but our very selves.

People: We offer to God our lives because we are God's people.

Hymns and Sacred Songs
"All People that on Earth Do Dwell"
found in:
UMH: 75
H82: 377/378
PH: 220/221
NNBH: 36
NCH: 7
CH: 18
LBW: 245

"Holy God, We Praise Thy Name"
found in:
UMH: 79
H82: 366
PH: 460
NCH: 276
LBW: 535

"We Gather Together"
found in:
UMH: 131
H82: 433
PH: 599
AAHH: 342
NNBH: 326
NCH: 421
CH: 276

"O Church of God, United"
found in:
UMH: 547

"Where Charity and Love Prevail"
found in:
UMH: 549
H82: 581
NCH: 396

"We Are the Church"
found in:
UMH: 558

"Go, Make of All Disciples"
found in:
UMH: 571

"O Zion, Haste"
found in:
UMH: 573
H82: 539
NNBH: 422
LBW: 397

Prayer for the Day / Collect
O God who calls your people into covenant: Grant us the grace to be faithful to you and to the neighbors you have entrusted to our care; through Jesus Christ our Savior. Amen.

OR

We come to worship and praise you, our God and Savior, because you desire our companionship. We come together to worship because you have made us one in Christ. Help us to love one another with such care and devotion that all may know you are present among us. Amen.

Prayer of Confession

Leader: Let us confess to God and before one another our sins and especially our failure to live faithfully in God's gracious covenant.

People: We confess to you, our Creator and our Redeemer, that we have failed to live within the bounds of the covenant you have so graciously offered to us. We have not centered our lives in you and your way, nor have we rightly offered you our praise and our lives. We have failed to care for one another as you have cared for us. Forgive us and empower us with your Spirit that we may live more faithfully in your image. Amen.

Leader: God is the faithful One who offers to us the covenant of grace again and again. Know that you are forgiven and restored to God's covenant once again.

Prayers of the People (and the Lord's Prayer)

We come together to offer our praise and worship to you, O God, because you have called us to be your people united in covenant to you and to one another. We praise you for your faithfulness and for your grace when we are unfaithful.

(The following paragraph may be used if a separate prayer of confession has not been used.)

We confess to you, our Creator and our Redeemer, that we have failed to live within the bounds of the covenant you have so graciously offered to us. We have not centered our lives in you and your way, nor have we rightly offered you our praise and our lives. We have failed to care for one another as you have cared for us. Forgive us and empower us with your Spirit that we may live more faithfully in your image. Amen.

In the hustle and bustle of our lives we often forget you, though you are the very life that flows within us. Yet you do not forget us. Creation itself speaks of regularity and faithfulness if we but look with the eyes of faith. We are truly blessed that you have called us your very own.

(Other thanksgivings may be offered.)
We offer into your presence and grace those who do not know your gracious ways. We pray for those who are trodden down and feel that there is no one to help them. We pray for those who are desperately looking for you and do not know how to find you. We pray for ourselves and our sisters and brothers that we may not only lift others in prayers but that we might lift them up to you in our words and in our deeds.

(Other intercessions may be offered.)
All these things we ask in the name of our Savior Jesus Christ who taught us to pray together saying:
Our Father... Amen.

(Or if the Lord's Prayer is not used at this point in the service)
All this we ask in the name of the Blessed and Holy Trinity. Amen.

Passion / Palm Sunday

Isaiah 50:4-9a
Philippians 2:5-11
Mark 14:1—15:47

Call to Worship
Palm emphasis
Leader: Let us give thanks to God who is good.
People: God's steadfast loves endures forever!
Leader: Enter the gates of righteousness and praise God!
People: Thanks be to God who answers us and saves us!
Leader: Give thanks to God who is always good!
People: God's steadfast loves endures forever!

OR

Passion emphasis
Leader: Be gracious to us, God, for we are in distress.
People: Our lives are spent with sorrow and sighing.
Leader: Our strength fails because of our misery.
People: We hear the whispering as they plot against us.
Leader: But we will trust in you, our God and our strength!
People: Let your face shine upon us; save us in your love!

Hymns and Sacred Songs
Palm emphasis
"All Glory, Laud and Honor"
found in:
UMH: 280
H82: 154/155
PH: 88
AAHH: 226

NNBH: 102
NCH: 216/217
CH: 192
LBW: 108

"Lift Up Your Heads, Ye Mighty Gates"
found in:
UMH: 213
H82: 436
PH: 8
NCH: 117
CH: 129
LBW: 32
Renew: 59

"Hosanna, Loud Hosanna"
found in:
UMH: 278
PH: 89
NCH: 213

"Ride On! Ride On in Majesty"
found in:
H82: 156
PH: 90/91
NCH: 215
CH: 191
LBW: 121

Passion emphasis
"Lift High the Cross"
found in:
UMH: 159
H82: 473
PH: 371

AAHH: 242
NCH: 198
CH: 108
LBW: 377
Renew: 297

"In the Cross of Christ I Glory"
found in:
UMH: 295
H82: 441/442
PH: 84
NNBH: 104
NCH: 193/194
LBW: 104

"What Wondrous Love Is This?"
found in:
UMH: 292
H82: 439
PH: 85
NCH: 223
CH: 200
LBW: 385
Renew: 277

"Ah, Holy Jesus"
found in:
UMH: 262
H82: 158
PH: 93
NCH: 218
CH: 210
LBW: 123
Renew: 183

"He Is Exalted"
found in:
CCB: 30
Renew: 238

"Only by Grace"
found in:
CCB: 42

Prayer for the Day / Collect
Palm emphasis
O God who comes in humility to face evil: Grant us the grace to truly join your parade and stand against the violence around us; through Jesus Christ our Savior. Amen.

Passion emphasis
O God whose life cannot be swallowed up in death: Grant us the faith to trust our lives into your care so that we may truly live as your children and as disciples of Jesus; through Jesus Christ our Savior. Amen.

Prayer of Confession
Leader: Let us confess to God and before one another our sins and especially the ways in which we fail to follow Jesus when the way becomes difficult.
People: We confess to you, O God, and before one another that we have sinned. We gladly come out for the parade when the crowd is for Jesus but we prefer to hide with the other disciples when things get ugly. We want to be liked, to be accepted. We fear standing up and being counted when it means being in the minority or even being alone. Forgive us our shallow commitments and empower us with the Spirit of Jesus that we may walk into our Jerusalems and face whatever is there. Amen.

Leader: God knows how difficult it is for us to stand out as being different or odd. Yet God created us to be unique and delights in our standing up for ourselves. Take courage and take your stand for the delight of God.

Prayers of the People (and the Lord's Prayer)

We praise and adore you, O God, for you are the one who comes among us to bring us life and not just existence. You come to show us how to resist evil and embrace the divine life of love and compassion.

(The following paragraph may be used if a separate prayer of confession has not been used.)
We confess to you, O God, and before one another that we have sinned. We gladly come out for the parade when the crowd is for Jesus but we prefer to hide with the other disciples when things get ugly. We want to be liked, to be accepted. We fear standing up and being counted when it means being in the minority or even being alone. Forgive us our shallow commitments and empower us with the Spirit of Jesus that we may walk into our Jerusalems and face whatever is there.

We give you thanks for the wonders of your love. We thank you for our homes and families but most of all we thank you for Jesus who came to be our guide and our Savior.

(Other thanksgivings may be offered.)
We look at our lives and the life of our world and we know how much we are in need of salvation. As you move among us and call us to your wholeness, help us to join you in bringing that wholeness to others.

(Other intercessions may be offered.)
All these things we ask in the name of our Savior Jesus Christ who taught us to pray together saying:

Our Father... Amen.

(Or if the Our Father is not used at this point in the service)
All this we ask in the name of the Blessed and Holy Trinity.
Amen.

Maundy Thursday

Exodus 12:1-4 (5-10) 11-14
1 Corinthians 11:23-26
John 13:1-17, 31b-35

Call to Worship

Leader: What shall we return to God for all God's goodness to us?

People: We shall lift the cup of salvation and call on God.

Leader: Precious in God's sight is the death of his beloved.

People: O God, we are your servants, the children of your servants.

Leader: Let us pay our vows to God in the presence of the congregation.

People: We will offer to God our sacrifice of thanksgiving.

OR

Leader: Come, for Jesus calls us to the wash basin.

People: We could never let Jesus wash our feet!

Leader: But Jesus calls and says it must be done.

People: Because of our love for Jesus, we will let it be done.

Leader: Come, for Jesus calls us to the wash basin.

People: But he has already washed our feet!

Leader: Yes, but now he wants you to wash each others' feet!

Hymns and Sacred Songs
"Of the Father's Love Begotten"
found in:

UMH: 184
PH: 309
NCH: 118
CH: 104
LBW: 42
Renew: 252

"You Satisfy the Hungry Heart"
found in:
UMH: 629
PH: 521
CH: 429

"Jesu, Jesu"
found in:
UMH: 432
H82: 602
PH: 367
NCH: 498
CH: 600
Renew: 289

"Make Me a Captive, Lord"
found in:
UMH: 421
PH: 378

"O the Depth of Love Divine"
found in:
UMH: 627

"Here, O My Lord, I See Thee"
found in:
UMH: 623
H82: 318

PH: 520
NCH: 336
CH: 416
LBW: 211

"One Bread, One Body"
found in:
UMH: 620
CH: 393

"For the Bread Which You Have Broken"
found in:
UMH: 614/615
H82: 340/341
PH: 508/509
CH: 411
LBW: 200

"Make Me a Servant"
found in:
CCB: 90

"Fill My Cup, Lord"
found in:
CCB: 47

Prayer for the Day / Collect

O God who comes to us as a slave: Grant us the grace to know your deepest love for us so that we may give our love for others as we serve them in their needs; through Jesus Christ our Savior. Amen.

OR

We come into your presence, O God, and ask that you would teach us once more about the humility of Jesus who knelt to serve. As he cares for us, empower us to boldly serve others in his name. Amen.

Prayer of Confession

Leader: Let us confess to God and before one another our sins and especially our reluctance to serve others as Christ has served us.

People: We confess to you, O God, and before one another that we have sinned. We are very good at ordering other people about and telling them what we need. We are not so comfortable serving others in humility. We prefer to be the host or the guest rather than the waitstaff. Like Peter we would pull Jesus up from his serving stance and place him at the seat of honor. We do not understand the power of love and service. Forgive us and teach us your love that serves in true compassion. Amen.

Leader: God serves us even in our selfishness and washes us so that we might learn to wash others. Receive the grace and love of God so that you may offer it to others.

Prayers of the People (and the Lord's Prayer)

We praise you, O God, in all your awesome power. We praise you as you display that power in acts of loving compassion and service.

(The following paragraph may be used if a separate prayer of confession has not been used.)

We confess to you, O God, and before one another that we have sinned. We are very good at ordering other people about and telling them what we need. We are not so comfortable serving others in humility. We prefer to be the host or the guest rather than the waitstaff. Like Peter we would pull Jesus up from his serving stance and place him at the seat of honor. We do not understand the power of love and service. Forgive us and teach us your love that serves in true compassion.

Our hearts are full of thanksgiving for all the ways in which you have come to us in compassion and cared for us in our needs. You have made the world to yield all the things we need for existence and for abundant life. You have offered yourself to us in service and in the humble elements of common bread and wine.

(Other thanksgivings may be offered.)
We pray for one another in our need and for all your creation that groans to know the completeness of your salvation. Grant that we may truly follow our Savior and serve the world until your reign is complete.

(Other intercessions may be offered.)
All these things we ask in the name of our Savior Jesus Christ who taught us to pray together saying:
Our Father... Amen.

(Or if the Our Father is not used at this point in the service)
All this we ask in the name of the Blessed and Holy Trinity. Amen.

Good Friday

Isaiah 52:13—53:12
Hebrews 10:16-25
John 18:1—19:42

N.B. The service of Tenebrae is a very moving time of reflecting on the Passion of our Lord. There are many resources available to help your congregation if you decide to include this in your Good Friday worship.

Call to Worship
Leader: My God, my God, why have you forsaken us?
People: Why are you so far from helping us, O God?
Leader: Yet God is holy, enthroned on the praises of God's people.
People: Our ancestors trusted in God and they were not disappointed.
Leader: It was God who plucked us from the womb.
People: It was God who kept us safe at our mother's breast.
Leader: Let us tell of God's name in the midst of the congregation!
People: We who fear God will praise God's holy name!

OR

Leader: Come and hear the good news of this day.
People: Jesus died today. What could be good about it?
Leader: Jesus' death was awful but we know the secret.
People: What could possibly turn this day to good?
Leader: Evil has overstepped its bounds. The story will not end today!

People: God's love will triumph! Love that sacrifices all will not be denied!

Hymns and Sacred Songs
"'Tis Finished! The Messiah Dies"
found in:
UMH: 282

"To Mock Your Reign, O Dearest Lord"
found in:
UMH: 285
H82: 170

"O Sacred Head, Now Wounded"
found in:
UMH: 286
H82: 168/169
PH: 98
AAHH: 250
NNBH: 108
NCH: 226
CH: 202
LBW: 116/117
Renew: 235

"He Never Said a Mumbalin' Word"
found in:
UMH: 291
PH: 95
CH: 208

"Beneath the Cross of Jesus"
found in:
UMH: 297
H82: 498

PH: 92
AAHH: 247
NNBH: 106
NCH: 190
CH: 197
LBW: 107

"Lord of the Dance"
found in:
UMH: 261

"Were You There?"
found in:
UMH: 288
H82: 172
PH: 102
AAHH: 254
NNBH: 109
NCH: 229
CH: 198
LBW: 92

"Jesus, Keep Me Near the Cross"
found in:
UMH: 301
NNBH: 103
NCH: 197
CH: 587

"O How He Loves You and Me"
found in:
CCB: 38
Renew: 27

"Only by Grace"
found in:
CCB: 42

Prayer for the Day / Collect
O God who withholds nothing to save your creation: Grant us the faith to live into the new life we are offered through Jesus Christ our Savior. Amen.

OR

We come to worship you, O God, who withholds nothing from us. You give your Son, your very self, to us so that we can be grasped by your love. Open us to your grace that we might truly receive the new life Christ offers us. Amen.

Prayer of Confession
Leader: Let us confess to God and before one another our sins and especially the ways in which we try to save ourselves rather than trusting in God's love.
People: We confess to you, O God, and before one another that we have sinned. We think we know the answers to life and how we can come out on top. We think we can use power and might and wealth like the world does and get different results. But we end up broken and lost when we do this. Forgive us our foolish ways and grant us the grace to live in your love so that, like Jesus, we may overcome all evil with good. Amen.
Leader: God desires our wholeness and healing. God comes among us even this day to offer it to us. Receive the power of God's Spirit to live in love and defeat the evil that is around us.

Prayers of the People (and the Lord's Prayer)
We come in awe and wonder before you, O God, because of

141

your great love, which leads you to come and die among us as one of us. Such love is too wondrous for us to understand. We can only kneel in humble gratefulness.

(The following paragraph may be used if a separate prayer of confession has not been used.)
We confess to you, O God, and before one another that we have sinned. We think we know the answers to life and how we can come out on top. We think we can use power and might and wealth like the world does and get different results. But we end up broken and lost when we do this. Forgive us our foolish ways and grant us the grace to live in your love so that, like Jesus, we may overcome all evil with good.

We give you thanks for all the blessings you have given us. There is no end to your caring for us and tending to us as the Good Shepherd. Most of all we thank you for the life and death of Jesus, which brings us to your great love.

(Other thanksgivings may be offered.)
We pray this day especially for those who feel estranged from you and have not experienced your love and compassion. As we meditate on your loving acts this day, quicken within us the love for others that we may share your grace with those around us.

(Other intercessions may be offered.)
All these things we ask in the name of our Savior Jesus Christ who taught us to pray together saying:
Our Father... Amen.

(Or if the Our Father is not used at this point in the service)
All this we ask in the name of the Blessed and Holy Trinity. Amen.

Easter Day

Acts 10:34-43
1 Corinthians 15:1-11
John 20:1-18

Call to Worship
Leader: Let us give thanks to God who is good.
People: God's steadfast love endures forever!
Leader: God is our strength and our might.
People: We are filled with songs of God's victory.
Leader: This day God has worked among us.
People: Let us rejoice in the mighty deeds of our God.

OR

Leader: We have experienced life that is like death.
People: We have known the pain of loss.
Leader: We wonder if there is any hope for us.
People: We wonder where to turn.
Leader: Today we hear the good news that God brings life from death.
People: Today we are reassured that God will triumph.
Leader: The resurrection of Jesus is our resurrection.
People: We are called to a new life in God.

Hymns and Sacred Songs
(Most of us have trouble fitting in the "favorites" on Easter so here are a few suggestions to add to your dilemma.)

"Hymn of Promise"
found in:
UMH: 707

"O God, Our Help in Ages Past"
found in:
UMH: 117
H82: 680
AAHH: 170
NNBH: 46
NCH: 25
CH: 67
LBW: 320

"Soon and Very Soon"
found in:
UMH: 706
AAHH: 193
NNBH: 476

"Easter People, Raise Your Voices"
found in:
UMH: 304

"Come, Ye Faithful, Raise the Strain"
found in:
UMH: 315
H82: 199/200
PH: 114/115
NCH: 230
CH: 215
LBW: 132

Prayer for the Day / Collect
O God who is life and is the source of our lives: Grant that as
you raised Jesus from death to new life so we may also find
new life in you; through Jesus Christ our Savior. Amen.

OR

We come to worship and praise you, O God, who has raised Jesus from the darkness of the tomb into the light of life eternal. Raise us with Jesus to new life that we may evermore praise and serve your holy name. Amen.

Prayer of Confession

Leader: Let us confess to God and before one another our sins and especially our willingness to choose death when God offers us life.

People: We confess that we are people who live a life that is more like death than anything else and yet we cling stubbornly to our path even as you offer us life that is abundant and full of meaning and peace. You offer us hope that is true and sure and yet we cling to our own delusions that we can save ourselves. Help us to let go of our misguided efforts to make our graves more comfortable and to turn to you for new life. Fill us with your Spirit that not only our lives will be vibrant but also that we will be sources of hope for others. Amen.

Leader: God desires nothing more than that we choose life over death. God forgives us and empowers us to live life fully by offering God's life to others.

Prayers of the People (and the Lord's Prayer)

We worship and adore you, God of life and blessing. You are not only the Creator of our lives but you are life itself.

(The following paragraph may be used if a separate prayer of confession has not been used.)

We confess that we are people who live a life that is more like death than anything else and yet we cling stubbornly to our path even as you offer us life that is abundant and full of meaning and peace. You offer us hope that is true and sure and yet we cling to our own delusions that we can save ourselves. Help us to let go of our misguided efforts to make our

145

graves more comfortable and to turn to you for new life. Fill us with your Spirit that not only our lives will be vibrant but also that we will be sources of hope for others.

We thank you for the breath of life that you have given to us so that we might have a share of your life. We rejoice at the good things you have given us and especially the true hope for eternal life through Jesus Christ our Savior.

(Other thanksgivings may be offered.)
We offer to your love and care those who struggle in death. Some are facing their own demise while others are grieving the loss of loved ones. Some are finding their bodies succumbing to the effects of death slowly overtaking them. Others are experiencing the death of relationships, hopes, and dreams. We pray that as you offer them new life in the midst of these things, our prayers, our words, and our deeds will be part of your ministry to them.

(Other intercessions may be offered.)
All these things we ask in the name of our Savior Jesus Christ who taught us to pray together saying:
Our Father... Amen.

(Or if the Lord's Prayer is not used at this point in the service)
All this we ask in the name of the Blessed and Holy Trinity. Amen.

Easter 2

Acts 4:32-35
1 John 1:1—2:2
John 20:19-31

Call to Worship
Leader: How good and pleasant it is when there is unity.
People: It is like anointing oil poured on the head.
Leader: It is like refreshing dew
People: that calls us to life anew.
Leader: This is the unity that Jesus prayed for
People: and that the Spirit opens up to us.

OR

Leader: Let us worship the God who created us,
People: who created us with minds to think and question.
Leader: Let us worship the God who created us,
People: who created us with the ability to know and experience.
Leader: Let us worship the God who loves us,
People: who loves us enough to hear our questions.

OR

Leader: Christ is risen! Alleluia!
People: Christ is risen indeed! Alleluia!
Leader: Christ is risen and is here among us!
People: We welcome the presence of our risen Christ!
Leader: Let us rejoice in the living presence of God among us!

People: We rejoice that the risen Christ brings us new life!

Hymns and Sacred Songs
"When Our Confidence Is Shaken"
found in:
UMH: 505
CH: 534

"Wellspring of Wisdom"
found in:
UMH: 506
CH: 596

"Joyful, Joyful, We Adore Thee"
found in:
UMH: 89
H82: 376
PH: 464
AAHH: 120
NNBH: 40
NCH: 4
CH: 2
LBW: 551

"God, Whose Love Is Reigning O'er Us"
found in:
UMH: 100

"God of Many Names"
found in:
UMH: 105
CH: 13

"Many Gifts, One Spirit"
found in:
UMH: 114
NCH: 177

"How Like a Gentle Spirit"
found in:
UMH: 115
NCH: 443
CH: 69

"Immortal, Invisible, God Only Wise"
found in:
UMH: 102
H82: 423
PH: 263
NCH: 1
CII: 66
LBW: 526

"God of the Sparrow, God of the Whale"
found in:
UMH: 122
PH: 272
NCH: 32
CH: 70

"Through It All"
found in:
UMH: 507
NNBH: 402
CH: 555

Prayer for the Day / Collect
O God who created us with minds and emotions: Grant that

we may trust your steadfast love enough to open our minds to think and our hearts to experience that love; through Jesus Christ our Savior. Amen.

OR

We come to worship you, risen Christ, and to find anew your love and life among and within us. We come to sing your praises and to listen for your instructions that we may take your living presence with us to the world you are saving. Amen.

Prayer of Confession
Leader: Let us confess to God and before one another our sins and especially our reluctance to know God and experience God with our whole being.
People: We confess to you, O God who created us, that we sometimes fear the gift of reasoning you have given us. We fear it at times in ourselves and especially in others. Because our thinking or experiencing you in new ways might make us uncomfortable, we hold on to what we have been told rather than what we know ourselves. Forgive us and give us the boldness of Thomas to know ourselves your loving and living presence among us. Amen.
Leader: God loves us and forgives us. God sends the Spirit among us and within us to make us bold and to give us new life. In the name of the risen Christ, you are forgiven and claimed by God.

Prayers of the People (and the Lord's Prayer)
We come to worship you in this glorious Easter season because you are the life who is not defeated by death but brings us life through the risen Christ.

(The following paragraph may be used if a separate prayer of confession has not been used.)

We confess to you, O God who created us, that we sometimes fear the gift of reasoning you have given us. We fear it at times in ourselves and especially in others. Because our thinking or experiencing you in new ways might make us uncomfortable, we hold on to what we have been told rather than what we know ourselves. Forgive us and give us the boldness of Thomas to know ourselves your loving and living presence among us.

We give you thanks for all your blessings, and we are most thankful for the presence of your risen Christ who comes to bring us life eternal and abundant. We thank you for all the ways we experience his life among us: in scripture, in sacrament, in each other, and the world around us.

(Other thanksgivings may be offered.)

We pray for those who are struggling and feel that they are stuck in death with no way out. We pray that as you come to them to bring them salvation, we might be part of your ministry to them. Use our love, our spirits, and our prayers; use our words, our deeds, and our gifts that they may know with us the glory of the risen Christ.

(Other intercessions may be offered.)

All these things we ask in the name of our Savior Jesus Christ who taught us to pray together saying:
Our Father... Amen.

(Or if the Lord's Prayer is not used at this point in the service)

All this we ask in the name of the Blessed and Holy Trinity. Amen.

Easter 3

Acts 3:12-19
1 John 3:1-7
Luke 24:36b-48

Call to Worship
Leader: Answer us when we call, O God!
People: God gave us room when we were in distress.
Leader: Be gracious to us and hear our prayer.
People: God hears when we call.
Leader: Let the light of your face shine on us, O God!
People: In you we find gladness and peace.

OR

Leader: God calls us to bring hope to the world.
People: We have little hope to offer from our lives.
Leader: God calls us to find our hope in the risen Christ.
People: It is the only source of hope we have in this world.
Leader: It is the only source of hope for the world, as well.
People: We will share our hope with the world, for it is the hope of God.

Hymns and Sacred Songs
"Come, Ye Faithful, Raise the Strain"
found in:
UMH: 315
H82: 199/200
PH: 114/115
NCH: 230
CH: 215
LBW: 132

"Hope of the World"
found in:
UMH: 178
H82: 472
PH: 360
NCH: 46
CH: 538
LBW: 493

"*Christo Vive*" ("Christ Is Risen")
found in:
UMH: 313
PH: 109
NCH: 235

"Hymn of Promise"
found in:
UMH: 707

"He Lives"
found in:
UMH: 310
AAHH: 275
NNBH: 119
CH: 226

"My Hope Is Built"
found in:
UMH: 368
PH: 379
AAHH: 385
NNBH: 274
NCH: 403
CH: 537
LBW: 293/294

"O Sons and Daughters, Let Us Sing"
found in:
UMH: 317
PH: 116/117
NCH: 244
CH: 220

"Christ Is Alive"
found in:
UMH: 318
H82: 182
PH: 108
LBW: 363

Prayer for the Day / Collect
O God who brings life from death and hope from despair: Grant us the faith to find in the risen Christ all the hope we need to face the uncertainty of life and to offer that hope to others; through Jesus Christ our Savior. Amen.

OR

We come to worship you, the God of life and resurrection, for you are the source of our lives and of our hopes. In your raising Jesus to new life, we find that we can be raised to new life as well. Help us to follow Jesus into new life and to give that new life to others. Amen.

Prayer of Confession
Leader: Let us confess to God and before one another our sins and especially how we take our eyes off the risen Christ, our hope, and see only the despair around us.
People: We confess to you, our God and Redeemer, and before our sisters and brothers that we have failed. We have failed to center our lives in the hope you bring us.

154

We have failed to turn a deaf ear to the call to feel despair and helplessness. We have failed to share with others the new life that we know you desire to give all your creation. Forgive us and empower us with the Spirit of the risen Christ that we may be signs of hope in this hopeless world. Amen.

Leader: God is hope and God has hope in you and for you. God is always ready to offer new life and new hope to you and to all creation. In the name of the risen Christ, you are forgiven and empowered to live the new life of disciples of Jesus.

Prayers of the People (and the Lord's Prayer)

We praise and worship you, O God, for you created life and have offered us a glorious future. You have envisioned a world where all are at peace and where healing is full and abundant.

(The following paragraph may be used if a separate prayer of confession has not been used.)

We confess to you, our God and Redeemer, and before our sisters and brothers that we have failed. We have failed to center our lives in the hope you bring us. We have failed to turn a deaf ear to the call to feel despair and helplessness. We have failed to share with others the new life that we know you desire to give all your creation. Forgive us and empower us with the Spirit of the risen Christ that we may be signs of hope in this hopeless world.

We give you thanks for all the ways in which hope has broken into our lives. We think of the miracle of birth and joy in memories of those whose physical presence is no longer with us. We remember the wonder of sunrises and the new days they bring.

(Other thanksgivings may be offered.)

155

We offer to your love those who have not found their hope in you. We see the sadness in their lives, in the desperate acts they seem driven to commit. We hear the flatness in the voices of those around us.

(Other intercessions may be offered.)
All these things we ask in the name of our Savior Jesus Christ who taught us to pray together saying:
Our Father... Amen.

(Or if the Lord's Prayer is not used at this point in the service)
All this we ask in the name of the Blessed and Holy Trinity. Amen.

Easter 4

Acts 4:5-12
1 John 3:16-24
John 10:11-18

Call to Worship
Leader: God is our shepherd
People: we have all that we need.
Leader: God brings us to pastures green and verdant.
People: By the still waters of refreshment, our God leads us.
Leader: Even when we walk in valleys of darkness,
People: the presence of God gives us peace.

OR

Leader: Jesus is our Good Shepherd.
People: We follow our shepherd who faithfully leads us.
Leader: Sometimes our way looks dark and dreary,
People: yet the presence of our shepherd comforts us.
Leader: Our shepherd invites us to care for and shepherd others.
People: We share the love of Jesus when we care for those in need.

Hymns and Sacred Songs
"He Leadeth Me, O Blessed Thought"
found in:
UMH: 128
AAHH: 142
NNBH: 235
CH: 545
LBW: 501

"The Lord's My Shepherd, I'll Not Want"
found in:
UMH: 136
PH: 170
CH: 78
LBW: 451

"The Lord Is My Shepherd"
found in:
AAHH: 426
NNBH: 241

"The Gift of Love"
found in:
UMH: 408
AAHH: 522
CH: 526

"Where Charity and Love Prevail"
found in:
UMH: 549
H82: 581
NCH: 396
LBW: 126

"Great Is Thy Faithfulness"
found in:
UMH: 140
PH: 276
AAHH: 158
NCH: 423
CH: 86

"Your Love, O God"
found in:

UMH: 120
CH: 71

"How Can We Name a Love?"
found in:
UMH: 111

"Lord God, Your Love Has Called Us Here"
found in:
UMH: 579

"God of Love and God of Power"
found in:
UMH: 578

"What Does the Lord Require?"
found in:
UMH: 441
H82: 605
PH: 405
CH: 659

"Jesu, Jesu"
found in:
UMH: 432
H82: 602
PH: 367
NCH: 498
CH: 600

"Give Thanks with a Grateful Heart"
found in:
Renew: 266

"Send Me, Jesus"
found in:
Renew: 308

"Psalm 91: On Eagle's Wings"
found in:
Renew: 112

"Our Love Belongs to You, O Lord" ("*Amarte Soloa ti, Senor*")
found in:
CCB: 63

"God, You Are My God"
found in:
CCB: 60

Prayer for the Day / Collect
O God who leads your people as a shepherd: Grant us the faith to follow your Son, our Good Shepherd, and to obey his command as we love and care for those in need through Jesus Christ our Savior. Amen.

OR

We come to worship you, our Good Shepherd, and to take our place with you in caring for those in need. Receive our praises and empower us to be faithful shepherds of all your people. Amen.

Prayer of Confession
Leader: Let us confess to God and before one another our sins and especially how we have neglected those in need whom God has entrusted to our care.

People: We confess to you and before one another the sins of our lives. We are very aware of our needs and wants and not so aware of the needs of others. We worry about the labels on our clothes when there are those who have no clothing at all. We worry about the tenderness of our steaks when others are starving to death. We cluck our tongues over the cost of our French artesian bottled water when others drink water so filthy we would not walk through it. We want the Good Shepherd to take care of all our wants and desires, but we overlook his command for us to take care of the needs of others. Forgive us, Good Shepherd, and make us as aware of the needs of others as we are of our own desires. By the power of your Spirit, bring us to the place where we gladly care for the needs of others even at the expense of our own needs. Make us true disciples of the One we call our Good Shepherd. Amen.

Leader: God, our Shepherd, knows our sins and our self-centeredness. God also knows the image in which we were created and we are being saved back into. God grant you forgiveness and the power of the Spirit to fulfill your prayers and to be faithful disciples of Jesus the Christ.

Prayers of the People (and the Lord's Prayer)

We praise and adore you, O God, for you are our Creator and our God; our lover and our guide; our Shepherd and our Judge. You created us in your image and have called us to shepherd those in need.

(The following paragraph may be used if a separate prayer of confession has not been used.)

We confess to you and before one another the sins of our lives. We are very aware of our needs and wants and not so aware of the needs of others. We worry about the labels on

161

our clothes when there are those who have no clothing at all. We worry about the tenderness of our steaks when others are starving to death. We cluck our tongues over the cost of our French artesian bottled water when others drink water so filthy we would not walk through it. We want the Good Shepherd to take care of all our wants and desires, but we overlook his command for us to take care of the needs of others. Forgive us, Good Shepherd, and make us as aware of the needs of others as we are of our own desires. By the power of your Spirit, bring us to the place where we gladly care for the needs of others even at the expense of our own needs. Make us true disciples of the One we call our Good Shepherd.

We give you thanks for all the blessings you have bestowed upon us. We thank you for your presence of peace in times of darkness and distress. We thank you for your presence of joy in times of goodness. We thank you for your presence in each and every kind deed we do for those we find in need.

(Other thanksgivings may be offered.)
We are very aware of the neediness of the world around us. We are bombarded with news of violence, hunger, and poverty. Even as we offer the hurts of the world into your caring hands, we pray for ourselves that we may be faithful disciples of Jesus who shepherd those around us.

(Other intercessions may be offered.)
All these things we ask in the name of our Savior Jesus Christ who taught us to pray together saying:
Our Father... Amen.

(Or if the Lord's Prayer is not used at this point in the service)
All this we ask in the name of the Blessed and Holy Trinity. Amen.

Easter 5

Acts 8:26-40
1 John 4:7-21
John 15:1-8

Call to Worship
Leader: All the ends of the earth shall remember and turn to God.
People: All the families of the nation shall worship before God.
Leader: Dominion belongs to God.
People: God rules over the nations.
Leader: Let us live for our God.
People: Let us proclaim God's deliverance forever.

OR

Leader: Let us open our lives to our Creator and Redeemer.
People: We offer our lives to the One who loves us.
Leader: God's care includes our pruning.
People: We are fearful and yet we trust in God.
Leader: Let us submit ourselves to the loving vinekeeper.
People: We are safe in the hands of the God of Jesus.

OR

Leader: Come and cast your fears on the God of love.
People: We want to hide and isolate ourselves from danger.
Leader: The God of perfect love invites you to leave your fears.
People: How can we not focus on the things that scare us?

Leader: Put you heart and minds on the things of God.
People: We will trade our fears for faith and service.

Hymns and Sacred Songs
"Give to the Winds Thy Fears"
found in:
UMH: 129
H82: 286
NCH: 404

"The Care the Eagle Gives Her Young"
found in:
UMH: 118
NCH: 468
CH: 76

"O God, Our Help in Ages Past"
found in:
UMH: 117
H82: 680
AAHH: 170
NNBH: 46
NCH: 25
CH: 68
LBW: 320

"Standing on the Promises"
found in:
UMH: 374
AAHH: 373
NNBH: 257
CH: 552

"Learning to Lean"
found in:
CCB: 74

"God Is so Good"
found in:
CCB: 75

Prayer for the Day / Collect

O God who is perfect love: Grant us the faith to believe in your love and to lose ourselves in loving service; through Jesus Christ our servant. Amen.

OR

O God who is the loving vinekeeper: Grant us the grace to offer to you those unyielding branches so that you may prune them away and free us for joyful service; through Jesus Christ our vine. Amen.

OR

We come to worship you, God of faithful love. Help us to offer to you our fears, those inside us and those around us. Give us such faith in you that we are bold to live into your reign and to share the good news of Jesus with the world. Amen.

Prayer of Confession

Leader: Let us confess to God and before one another our sins and especially the fears that we harbor inside.
People: We confess to you, O God, and before our sisters and brothers that we are afraid. We are afraid of who we might truly be, and we are afraid of those around us. We do not trust ourselves, others, or you. Forgive us our

distrust and fear and so endow us with your Spirit that we will be filled with faith to face ourselves and others in the sure and certain knowledge of your love and care. **Amen.**

Leader: God hears our prayers and bids us not to fear. By the power of the Spirit know you are forgiven and given a new opportunity to leave your fears in the hands of Jesus.

Prayers of the People (and the Lord's Prayer)
We adore you, God of love and faithfulness. You alone live in the fullness of your true being. You are love and you are faithful to yourself. That makes you One we can trust.

(The following paragraph may be used if a separate prayer of confession has not been used.)
We confess to you, O God, and before our sisters and brothers that we are afraid. We are afraid of who we might truly be, and we are afraid of those around us. We do not trust ourselves, others, or you. Forgive us our distrust and fear and so endow us with your Spirit that we will be filled with faith to face ourselves and others in the sure and certain knowledge of your love and care.

We give you thanks for all the ways in which you have shared your love and care with us. We thank you for creation and for families. We thank you for the ways in which you allow others to bring your love to us through their physical presence.

(Other thanksgivings may be offered.)
We offer up to your never-ending love the cares of our hearts and the hurts of your creation. As you reach out in faithful caring, help us to be part of your ministry to those in need.

(Other intercessions may be offered.)
All these things we ask in the name of our Savior Jesus Christ

who taught us to pray together saying:
Our Father... Amen.

(Or if the Lord's Prayer is not used at this point in the service)
All this we ask in the name of the Blessed and Holy Trinity.
Amen.

Easter 6

Acts 10:44-48
1 John 5:1-6
John 15:9-17

Call to Worship
Leader: O sing to God a new song,
People: for our God has done marvelous things.
Leader: God's right hand and holy arm have provided victory.
People: God has remembered steadfast love and faithfulness.
Leader: Let the floods clap their hands;
People: let the hills sing for joy at the presence of our God.

OR

Leader: The God who is steadfast love calls us to worship.
People: We offer our praise to the God whose love never fails.
Leader: God calls us to worship and to fulfill God's image.
People: We ask God to help us become a more loving people.
Leader: God's love is more than feeling. It is active sacrifice.
People: We pray for God's grace to offer ourselves in love for others.

Hymns and Sacred Songs
"God of Grace and God of Glory"
found in:
UMH: 577

H82: 594/595
PH: 420
NCH: 436
CH: 464
LBW: 415

"Lord, Speak to Me"
found in:
UMH: 463
PH: 426
NCH: 531
LBW: 403

"Make Me a Captive, Lord"
found in:
UMH: 421
PH: 378

"*Cuando El Pobre*" ("When the Poor Ones")
found in:
UMH: 434
PH: 407
CH: 662

"Must Jesus Bear the Cross Alone"
found in:
UMH: 424
AAHH: 554
NNBH: 221

"Lord God, Your Love Has Called Us Here"
found in:
UMH: 579

"Rescue the Perishing"
found in:
UMH: 591
NNBH: 414

Prayer for the Day / Collect
O God of steadfast love: Grant that we may follow our Savior Jesus and offer ourselves in love and care for others; through the same Jesus Christ. Amen.

OR

We come to worship you, our God and our Savior, and to ask your grace and Spirit to so fill us that we may go out in the power of your love to give ourselves for others. Amen.

Prayer of Confession
Leader: Let us confess to God and before one another our sins and especially how we avoid sacrificing in love for others.
People: We confess to you and before one another the sins of our lives and especially the self-centeredness of our lives. We profess to be disciples of Jesus, but unlike him, we avoid those places where we are called to make sacrifices for others. We find it difficult to offer a dollar to a beggar on the streets. We are certainly not willing to die for dirty beggars. We are quick to find someone to blame, usually the person who needs us, rather than to find some way to help them. Forgive us and give us the Spirit of Jesus that we may follow him more faithfully and truly offer ourselves for others in his name. Amen.
Leader: God is the One who loves us and all creation with a love that knows no bounds. God grant you forgiveness of your sins and the power to amend your lives and to live faithfully as disciples of Jesus.

Prayers of the People (and the Lord's Prayer)

We praise and adore you, O God, for you are the one whose steadfast love is from everlasting to everlasting. You hold your creation in loving hands and offer your own life to bring life to us. You breathe within us your own breath.

(The following paragraph may be used if a separate prayer of confession has not been used.)

We confess to you and before one another the sins of our lives and especially the self-centeredness of our lives. We profess to be disciples of Jesus, but unlike him, we avoid those places where we are called to make sacrifices for others. We find it difficult to offer a dollar to a beggar on the streets. We are certainly not willing to die for dirty beggars. We are quick to find someone to blame, usually the person who needs us, rather than to find some way to help them. Forgive us and give us the Spirit of Jesus that we may follow him more faithfully and truly offer ourselves for others in his name.

We give you thanks for all the ways your love has been known to us. We thank you for the ways in which you dwell within your creation and speak to us of your never-ending care for us and all you have created.

(Other thanksgivings may be offered.)

Because you are the God who loves, we offer to you the cares of our hearts. We know your concern for us and for the cares we bring with us to worship. We know your concern for the hurts and ills of all your people. Grant us the grace to follow the example of our Savior Jesus and offer ourselves for the healing of others.

(Other intercessions may be offered.)

All these things we ask in the name of our Savior Jesus Christ who taught us to pray together saying:

Our Father... Amen.

(Or if the Lord's Prayer is not used at this point in the service)
All this we ask in the name of the Blessed and Holy Trinity.
Amen.

Ascension of Our Lord / Easter 7

Acts 1:1-11
Ephesians 1:15-23
Luke 24:44-53

Call to Worship
Leader: Clap your hands, all God's people.
People: Shout to God with songs of joy!
Leader: For God, the Most High, is awesome.
People: God reigns over all creation.
Leader: Sing praises to God.
People: Sing praises, for God is highly exalted.

OR

Leader: God has called us to be peculiar people.
People: Who does God want us to be?
Leader: God is creating us to the fullness of Christ.
People: We have an awesome responsibility!
Leader: The God who raised the Christ will empower you.
People: Come, Holy Spirit, and fill us with yourself.

Hymns and Sacred Songs
"Source and Sovereign, Rock and Cloud"
found in:
UMH: 113
CII: 12

"Filled with the Spirit's Power"
found in:
UMH: 537
NCH: 266
LBW: 160

"O Breath of Life"
found in:
UMH: 543
CH: 250

"The Church's One Foundation"
found in:
UMH: 545/546
H82: 525
PH: 442
AAHH: 337
NNBH: 297
NCH: 386
LBW: 369

"All Praise to Our Redeeming Lord"
found in:
UMH: 554

"Lord, Whose Love Through Humble Service"
found in:
UMH: 581

"As the Deer Pants for the Water"
found in:
Renew: 9

"Emmanuel"
found in:
Renew: 28

"Sent by the Lord"
found in:
Renew: 154

"May the Mind of Christ, My Savior"
found in:
Renew: 285

"Send Us Out"
found in:
Renew: 304

Prayer for the Day / Collect

O God who created all that is and was and ever shall be: Grant that we may truly be so filled with the Spirit of Christ that we shall be the fullness of the One who fills all in all; through Jesus Christ our Savior. Amen.

OR

We come to worship you, O God, and be filled with the power and grace of the risen Christ. Open our minds to understand what you desire for the salvation of your creation and open our hearts to be empowered to carry out your work. Amen.

Prayer of Confession

Leader: Let us confess to God and before one another our sins and especially the ways in which we fail to be the presence of our risen Christ.

People: We confess to you, O God, and before our sisters and brothers that we have failed to be your obedient church. We have looked for ways to lift up ourselves and our local institution, but we have failed to seek to be your presence in this community and in the world. We have been more concerned about our own security than about the salvation of your children. Forgive us and so empower us with the Spirit of the risen Christ that we may truly be the fullness of your presence to all your children. Amen.

Leader: God loves us and all of creation with a love that never ends. God grants us forgiveness and desires nothing more than to fill us with the Spirit and claim all creation for God's own.

Prayers of the People (and the Lord's Prayer)
We worship and adore you, O God, for there is none like you. Our language and images point to your awesome being, but we cannot do you justice. You are beyond our imagination and beyond our praise. Yet you are the One who comes to dwell within us and among us. You made us in your image and desire to have your fullness revealed in and through us.

(The following paragraph may be used if a separate prayer of confession has not been used.)
We confess to you, O God, and before our sisters and brothers that we have failed to be your obedient church. We have looked for ways to lift up ourselves and our local institution, but we have failed to seek to be your presence in this community and in the world. We have been more concerned about our own security than about the salvation of your children. Forgive us and so empower us with the Spirit of the risen Christ that we may truly be the fullness of your presence to all your children.

We give you thanks for all the ways in which your love and grace have been made known to us. We are especially thankful for those who have allowed themselves to be used as channels of your love and grace. We thank you for the way that even mute creation sings your glory.

(Other thanksgivings may be offered.)
We offer to your love and care the hurts and needs of this world. We are frighteningly aware of our responsibility to not only pray for these but to bring your presence, grace, and power to them.

176

(Other intercessions may be offered.)
All these things we ask in the name of our Savior Jesus Christ
who taught us to pray together saying:
Our Father... Amen.

*(Or if the Lord's Prayer is not used at this point in the
service)*
All this we ask in the name of the Blessed and Holy Trinity.
Amen.

Pentecost Sunday

Acts 2:1-21
Romans 8:22-27
John 15:26-27; 16:4b-15

Call to Worship
Leader: O God, how manifold are your works!
People: In wisdom you have made them all.
Leader: The earth is full of your creatures.
People: You have made creatures great and small.
Leader: They look to you for their food.
People: When you open your hand they are filled with good things.
Leader: When you hide your face, they are dismayed.
People: When you take away their breath, they die.

OR

Leader: God calls us into worship together, as Christ's body.
People: We come in all our differences of body and mind.
Leader: Bring the uniqueness of yourself and your heritage.
People: We come to share ourselves with each other and with God.
Leader: God delights in the glorious variety we represent in creation.
People: We give God thanks for all we learn from each other.

Hymns and Sacred Songs
(This could be a good opportunity to sing a hymn from

another language or tradition that the congregation hasn't attempted before.)

"All Creatures of Our God and King"
found in:
UMH: 62
H82: 400
PH: 455
AAHH: 147
NNBH: 33
NCH: 17
CH: 22
LBW: 527

"All Things Bright and Beautiful"
found in:
UMH: 147
H82: 405
PH: 267
NCH: 31
CH: 61

"In Christ There Is No East or West"
found in:
UMH: 548
H82: 529
PH: 439/440
AAHH: 398/399
NNBH: 299
NCH: 394/395
CH: 687
LBW: 259

"Forward Through the Ages"
found in:
UMH: 555
NCH: 377

"Help Us Accept Each Other"
found in:
UMH: 560
PH: 358
NCH: 388
CH: 487

"Send Us Out"
found in:
Renew: 304

"Behold, What Manner of Love"
found in:
CCB: 44

"I Am Loved"
found in:
CCB: 80

"Live in Charity"
found in:
CCB: 71

Prayer for the Day / Collect
O God who created all creatures great and small: Help us to celebrate who we are and to delight in the diversity others bring to your church; through Jesus Christ our Savior. Amen.

OR

We come into your presence, O God, in all our diversity. Even where we seem to be very similar we know there are glorious differences in your church around the world. We don't all look alike, sound alike, or even worship alike. But we are all your children, disciples of Jesus. Grant us the wisdom to celebrate our differences and to learn from them. Amen.

Prayer of Confession

Leader: Let us confess to God and before one another our sins and especially the ways in which we try to restrict the breadth of God's creation and reign.

People: **We confess to you, our Creator God and our Redeemer, that we have sinned against you and your creation in dividing ourselves up into factions and groups and then putting labels on each other: acceptable or unacceptable; loved or hated; trusted or scary. Forgive us our foolishness in missing the blessing of the diversity of your creation. Forgive us the foolishness of missing the blessing of the diversity of your church. Help us to see the risen Christ in all our sisters and brothers and to learn from them, rather than trying to form them into our image. Amen.**

Leader: God created us to delight in us. God loves us and forgives us and invites us to go forth as new creatures who celebrate their own uniqueness and the diversity of all creation.

Prayers of the People (and the Lord's Prayer)

We worship and adore you, O God, because you have created all that is in a wondrous display of diversity and joy. We stand in awe of the great whales as they leap and play in your ocean and we laugh at the antics of kittens and puppies. We see the beauty of the Grand Canyon and the beauty of tiny organisms under a microscope.

(The following paragraph may be used if a separate prayer of confession has not been used.)
We confess to you, our Creator God and our Redeemer, that we have sinned against you and your creation in dividing ourselves up into factions and groups and then putting labels on each other: acceptable or unacceptable; loved or hated; trusted or scary. Forgive us our foolishness in missing the blessing of the diversity of your creation. Forgive us the foolishness of missing the blessing of the diversity of your church. Help us to see the risen Christ in all our sisters and brothers and to learn from them, rather than trying to form them into our image.

We give you thanks for all the ways in which you come to us and teach us about yourself. We give you thanks for family, friends, and strangers who have taught us about you in lessons, in example, and in books. You have given us many ways to experience you and to express our praise and worship of you.

(Other thanksgivings may be offered.)
We pray for all your creation and especially for those who feel shunned and left out of your love because of the way your children treat them. As you draw them to yourself, so fill us with your love and compassion that we might be the means of sharing your grace with them.

(Other intercessions may be offered.)
All these things we ask in the name of our Savior Jesus Christ who taught us to pray together saying:
Our Father... Amen.

(Or if the Lord's Prayer is not used at this point in the service)

All this we ask in the name of the Blessed and Holy Trinity. Amen.

Holy Trinity Sunday

Isaiah 6:1-8
Romans 8:12-17
John 3:1-17

Call to Worship
Leader: Ascribe to God glory and strength.
People: Ascribe to God the glory due God's name.
Leader: The voice of God causes the oaks to whirl.
People: In God's temple, all cry, "Glory!"
Leader: May God give us strength.
People: May God bless us with peace!

OR

Leader: God calls us into worship.
People: We answer God's call and we offer our praise.
Leader: God calls us into relationship.
People: We answer God's call and unite with God and God's people.
Leader: God calls us into service.
People: We answer God's call and go out to be the body of Christ.

Hymns and Sacred Songs
"Here I Am, Lord"
found in:
UMH: 593
PH: 525
AAHH: 567
CH: 452

"Dear Jesus, in Whose Life I See"
found in:
UMH: 468

"Send Me, Lord"
found in:
UMH: 497
CH: 447

"Heralds of Christ"
found in:
UMH: 567

"O Zion, Haste"
found in:
UMH: 573
H82: 539
NNBH: 422
LBW: 397

"Whom Shall I Send?"
found in:
UMH: 582

"*Sois la Semilla*" ("You Are the Seed")
found in:
UMH: 583
NCH: 528
CH: 478

"Lord, You Give the Great Commission"
found in:
UMH: 584
H82: 528

AAHH: 429
CH: 469

Prayer for the Day / Collect
O God who speaks and worlds come into being: Grant us the grace to realize your voice, which does not command but, rather, invites us to become the bearers of your Spirit into your creation; through Jesus Christ our Savior. Amen.

OR

We come to worship you, our God who calls us into being. We come in answer to your voice and we offer ourselves to do your bidding. Fill us once again with your Spirit that we may truly be your presence for a world that desperately needs your healing touch. Amen.

Prayer of Confession
Leader: Let us confess to God and before one another our sins and especially the ways in which we fail to respond to God's call to be in mission.
People: God, we confess to you and before one another that we have sinned. We have sinned in more ways than we care to admit and we are painfully aware that we have avoided the opportunities where you have called us to be your witness, your presence, and your saving grace. We are so ready to receive your grace and so slow to offer it to others. Forgive us and so fill us with your Spirit that we may be more aware of your voice calling us to go and be about your work. Amen.
Leader: God loves us and hears us when we pray. God desires nothing more than to wrap all creation in the divine arms of loving kindness. Know that you are forgiven and granted to a new opportunity to be part of sharing God's grace and peace.

Prayers of the People (and the Lord's Prayer)

We worship and adore you, our Creator God, who spoke and the worlds came into being. You still speak and people go out to be your presence and grace for others.

(The following paragraph may be used if a separate prayer of confession has not been used.)
God we confess to you and before one another that we have sinned. We have sinned in more ways than we care to admit and we are painfully aware that we have avoided the opportunities where you have called us to be your witness, your presence, and your saving grace. We are so ready to receive your grace and so slow to offer it to others. Forgive us and so fill us with your Spirit that we may be more aware of your voice calling us to go and be about your work.

We give you thanks for all those who have heard your call and became your loving presence for us. You called folks to reach out and minister to us in our need. You called people who shared the good news about Jesus and through them we heard you call us to be disciples.

(Other thanksgivings may be offered.)
We offer to your loving care those who are in need of your healing and wholeness. We offer ourselves to be the bearers of that ministry to them.

(Other intercessions may be offered.)
All these things we ask in the name of our Savior Jesus Christ who taught us to pray together saying:
Our Father... Amen.

(Or if the Our Father is not used at this point in the service)
All this we ask in the name of the Blessed and Holy Trinity. Amen.

Proper 5
Pentecost 2
Ordinary Time 10

1 Samuel 8:4-11 (12-15) 16-20 (11:14-15)
2 Corinthians 4:13—5:1
Mark 3:20-35

Call to Worship
Leader: Let us give thanks to God with all our hearts.
People: We give your thanks, O God, for your steadfast love and faithfulness.
Leader: Though we walk in the way of trouble, God preserves us.
People: God reaches out and delivers us with love and grace.
Leader: God's purpose will come to fruition in us.
People: God's love endures forever and will never forsake us.

OR

Leader: Come and acknowledge that God alone is our sovereign.
People: God is God and God alone holds sway over us.
Leader: Do not be led astray by those who hold power.
People: God is the only true power, the only true leader for us.
Leader: God's claim and love for us surpasses all claims.
People: We heartily yield to God's loving claim on our lives.

Hymns and Sacred Songs
"Come, Thou Almighty King"
found in:
UMH: 61
H82: 365
PH: 139
AAHH: 327
NNBH: 38
NCH: 275
CH: 27
LBW: 522

"O Worship the King"
found in:
UMH: 73
H82: 388
PH: 476
NNBH: 6
NCH: 26
CH: 17
LBW: 548

"Praise the Lord Who Reigns Above"
found in:
UMII: 96
Renew: 253

"Immortal, Invisible, God Only Wise"
found in:
UMH: 103
H82: 423
PH: 263
NCH: 1
CH: 66

LBW: 526
Renew: 46

"Joyful, Joyful, We Adore Thee"
found in:
UMH: 89
H82: 376
PH: 464
AAHH: 120
NNBH: 40
NCH: 4
CH: 2
LBW: 551

"O God, Our Help in Ages Past"
found in:
UMH: 117
H82: 680
AAHH: 170
NNBH: 46
NCH: 25
CH: 67
LBW: 320

"Christ, Whose Glory Fills the Skies"
found in:
UMH: 173
H82: 6/7
PH: 462/463
LBW: 265

"O for a Thousand Tongues to Sing"
found in:
UMH: 57

H82: 493
PH: 466
AAHH: 184
NNBH: 23
NCH: 42
CH: 5
LBW: 559
Renew: 32

"All Hail King Jesus!"
found in:
CCB: 29
Renew: 35

"Lord, I Lift Your Name on High"
found in:
CCB: 36
Renew: 4

Prayer for the Day / Collect

O God who alone holds sway over all creation: Grant us the grace and faith to offer to you our devotion, allegiance, and praise; through Jesus Christ our Savior. Amen.

OR

We have come into your presence, O God, to worship you and to offer to you our true allegiance. It is only from you that we have received life and it is only to you that we offer the devotion of our lives. Fill us this day with your Spirit and the joy of your salvation. Amen.

Prayer of Confession

Leader: Let us confess to God and before one another our sins and especially the ways we look to others to save us.

People: **We confess to you, O God, and before one another that we have sinned. Like your people of old, we clamor for a person to lead us. Yet you alone are our sovereign and our guide. You alone hold the keys to life that is full, abundant, and eternal. Forgive us and call us back to serving you as we follow our Savior Jesus. Amen.**

Leader: God rules over us in love and faithfulness. God welcomes us back and desires nothing more than our own good, our own salvation. Know the love and forgiveness of God in your life as you live under the care and grace of our God.

Prayers of the People (and the Lord's Prayer)

We worship and adore you, O God, because you are the sovereign of the universe. You created us and you, alone, can lead us to salvation.

(The following paragraph may be used if a separate prayer of confession has not been used.)

We confess to you, O God, and before one another that we have sinned. Like your people of old, we clamor for a person to lead us. Yet you alone are our sovereign and our guide. You alone hold the keys to life that is full, abundant, and eternal. Forgive us and call us back to serving you as we follow our Savior Jesus.

We give you thanks for all the ways in which you have been faithful to us. You have walked beside us throughout our lives and have never failed to share your love with us. You have always owned us as your people even when we failed to acknowledge you as our God.

(Other thanksgivings may be offered.)

We pray for one another in our need and for all your creation as it groans with desire for its salvation.

(Other intercessions may be offered.)
All these things we ask in the name of our Savior Jesus Christ
who taught us to pray together saying:
Our Father... Amen.

(Or if the Our Father is not used at this point in the service)
All this we ask in the name of the Blessed and Holy Trinity.
Amen.

Proper 6
Pentecost 3
Ordinary Time 11

1 Samuel 15:34—16:13
2 Corinthians 5:6-10 (11-13) 14-17
Mark 4:26-34

Call to Worship
Leader: May God answer us when we call.
People: May the God of Jacob protect us.
Leader: May God grant you your heart's desire.
People: May God help you fulfill all your plans.
Leader: Some take pride in things of power.
People: But our joy is in the name of God.

OR

Leader: God calls us to change the world into God's reign.
People: We are few in number and power.
Leader: God created little seeds that become mighty plants.
People: Can we grow into a mighty force?
Leader: God is our Creator. We are a mighty force.
People: We will seek to use our small words and gestures for great things with God.

Hymns and Sacred Songs
"All Creatures of Our God and King"
found in:
UMH: 62
H82: 400
PH: 455
AAHH: 147

NNBH: 33
NCH: 17
CH: 22
LBW: 527

"How Great Thou Art"
found in:
UMH: 77
PH: 467
AAHH: 148
NNBH: 43
CH: 33
LBW: 532

"God of the Sparrow, God of the Whale"
found in:
UMH: 122
PH: 272
NCH: 32
CH: 70

"Many and Great, O God"
found in:
UMH: 148
H82: 385
PH: 271
NCH: 3
CH: 58

"*Tu Has Venido a la Orilla*" ("Lord, You Have Come to the Lakeshore")
UMH: 344
PH: 377
CH: 342

"Thy Word Is a Lamp"
found in:
UMH: 601
CH: 326

"Lord, Be Glorified"
found in:
CCB: 62

"Open Our Eyes, Lord" (especially v. 2)
found in:
CCB: 77

Prayer for the Day / Collect
O God who created the oak to come forth from an acorn: Grant us the faith to trust that your reign will come as we are faithful in the small words and acts of love and mercy that you call us to do; through Jesus Christ our Savior. Amen.

OR

We come to worship our God and our Savior and to be filled with the Spirit so that in all the things we do and say, even though they seem quite small, we might find ourselves part of God's reclaiming the world. Amen.

Prayer of Confession
Leader: Let us confess to God and before one another our sins and especially the ways in which we avoid doing what we can because it does not seem adequate.
People: We confess to you, O God, and before our sisters and brothers that we have failed to follow Jesus as he has called us to. We have hid behind the excuse that we are not influential enough, rich enough, or famous enough to make a real difference for God. We forget how God makes

so many large plants to grow from such little seeds. We forget how time and time again God chooses the smallest, the youngest, and the most unlikely to accomplish great things. Forgive us our foolish ways and help us to act boldly even when the act seems way too small to be significant. Fill us with the power of your Spirit that we might join our Savior in claiming the world for your reign. Amen.

Leader: God desires to reign in all creation. That includes our little lives. God loves us and forgives us and empowers us to live as part of God's great reign.

Prayers of the People (and the Lord's Prayer)

We offer you our praise and worship, God of all creation. You made the universe so vast and complex as well as the tiniest particle of an atom. You called of this good, the little as well as the great.

(The following paragraph may be used if a separate prayer of confession has not been used.)

We confess to you, O God, and before our sisters and brothers that we have failed to follow Jesus as he has called us to. We have hid behind the excuse that we are not influential enough, rich enough, or famous enough to make a real difference for God. We forget how God makes so many large plants to grow from such little seeds. We forget how time and time again God chooses the smallest, the youngest, and the most unlikely to accomplish great things. Forgive us our foolish ways and help us to act boldly even when the act seems way too small to be significant. Fill us with the power of your Spirit that we might join our Savior in claiming the world for your reign.

We thank you for all the ways in which we have experienced you and your loving kindness. We thank you for the small acts you called people to do that made such a large impact on our lives. We thank you for the word that may have seemed like an offhand remark to the one who made it but that created such a major impression on us.

(Other thanksgivings may be offered.)
We pray for those who feel they are too small and insignificant to matter to you or to anyone else. We pray that we may be part of your work in letting them know they are very important to you. We pray for ourselves and others that we may not be discouraged by the little we can do but made bold to do it all in your name.

(Other intercessions may be offered.)
All these things we ask in the name of our Savior Jesus Christ who taught us to pray together saying:
Our Father... Amen.

(Or if the Our Father is not used at this point in the service)
All this we ask in the name of the Blessed and Holy Trinity. Amen.

Proper 7
Pentecost 4
Ordinary Time 12

1 Samuel 17:(1a, 4-11, 19-23) 32-49
2 Corinthians 6:1-13
Mark 4:35-41

Call to Worship
Leader: God is a stronghold for the oppressed,
People: a stronghold in times of trouble.
Leader: Those who know God, trust in God.
People: God does not forsake those who seek God's presence.
Leader: The needy shall not always be forgotten,
People: nor the hope of the poor perish forever.

OR

Leader: God calls us to join in co-creating the reign of God.
People: We have heard God's call and are ready to follow.
Leader: The work of God lays before us.
People: But which is the work of God and which of mortals?
Leader: Let us listen for God's direction as we pray and worship.
People: We come to hear God so that we may obey God.

OR

Leader: Jesus knew God to be a parent, like a gracious father.

People: In Jesus we have come to know God as our loving parent.

Leader: God is like the mother eagle and the prodigal father.

People: God is tender and compassionate; God teaches and leads us.

Leader: Let us celebrate those who have been our earthly fathers and those who have been like fathers to us.

People: We rejoice in the way God's love and presence has been made known through them.

Hymns and Sacred Songs
"Of the Father's Love Begotten"
found in:
UMH: 184
PH: 309
NCH: 118
CH: 104
LBW: 42

"This Is My Father's World"
found in:
UMH: 144
H82: 651
PH: 293
AAHH: 149
NNBH: 41
CH: 59
LBW: 554

"Stand Up, Stand Up for Jesus"
found in:
UMH: 514
H82: 561
AAHH: 476

NNBH: 409
CH: 613
LBW: 389

"The Care the Eagle Gives Her Young"
found in:
UMH: 118
NCH: 468
CH: 76

"Our Parent, by Whose Name"
found in:
UMH: 447
LBW: 357

"What Does the Lord Require?"
found in:
UMH: 441
H82: 605
PH: 405
CH: 659

"The Voice of God Is Calling"
found in:
UMH: 436
CH: 666

"O Master, Let Me Walk with Thee"
found in:
UMH: 430
H82: 659/660
PH: 357
NNBH: 445
NCH: 503

CH: 602
LBW: 492

"Open Our Eyes, Lord"
found in:
CCB: 77

"Your Love Is Changing the World"
Renew: 287

Prayer for the Day / Collect
O God who has become incarnate in this world: Grant
that we may join you in calling your creation to its fullest
completion; through Jesus Christ our Savior. Amen.

OR

O God who suckles the young and welcomes back the
wayward: Grant that we may rejoice in your love shared
through human fathers and father figures and share your love
with others; through Jesus Christ our Savior. Amen.

OR

God of love and gracious kindness, help us to celebrate
your care for us in and through our fathers and those who
have been like fathers to us. Help us to remember that they
are reflections of your love but their failures belong to us
as mortals and do not reflect your steadfastness. Enable us
to be inspired by them and moved to share your love with
others. Amen.

Prayer of Confession
Leader: Let us confess to God and before one another our

sins and especially the way in which we assume that our side of the issue is God's.

People: We confess to you, our God and Redeemer, and before one another that we have sinned. We have failed to live up to your standards for our lives, and so we have missed the joy and blessings of life that you have offered. We have acted rashly and without consulting you. We think that the opinions and convictions we have are yours without testing them first against the message and life of Jesus. Forgive us and call us once again to sit at the feet of our Master and learn about you and your hopes and dreams for creation. Fill us with your Spirit that we may share together in bringing your reign to glorious flower. Amen.

Leader: God is gracious and kind, a loving parent forever, who does not forsake us or leave us to our sinfulness. God forgives us and grants us the power of the Spirit to go forth and claim all creation for the reign of God.

Prayers of the People (and the Lord's Prayer)
We praise and worship you, O God, for all the glories of your name. You are great and wondrous in power and glory, and yet you are tender and merciful with your creatures.

(The following paragraph may be used if a separate prayer of confession has not been used.)
We confess to you, our God and Redeemer, and before one another that we have sinned. We have failed to live up to your standards for our lives, and so we have missed the joy and blessings of life that you have offered. We have acted rashly and without consulting you. We think that the opinions and convictions we have are yours without testing them first against the message and life of Jesus. Forgive us and call us once again to sit at the feet of our Master and learn about you and your hopes and dreams for creation. Fill us with your

Spirit that we may share together in bringing your reign to glorious flower.

We thank you for all the ways you have made your love known to us and especially this day in the ways that folks have been fathers to us. You gave us biological fathers but you have also given us others, both male and female, who have helped fulfill that role for us. No one person can fully reflect your love for us, and so you give us multiple people to help us find your love.

(Other thanksgivings may be offered.)
We pray for those who have the responsibility of fatherhood. Fill them with your love and grace that they may be faithful reflections of you.

(Other intercessions may be offered.)
All these things we ask in the name of our Savior Jesus Christ who taught us to pray together saying:
Our Father... Amen.

(Or if the Lord's Prayer is not used at this point in the service)
All this we ask in the name of the Blessed and Holy Trinity. Amen.

Proper 8
Pentecost 5
Ordinary Time 13

2 Samuel 1:1, 17-27
2 Corinthians 8:7-15
Mark 5:21-43

Call to Worship
Leader: Out of the depths we cry to God.
People: Let your ears hear our cries.
Leader: If you mark iniquities, O God, who could stand?
People: But in God we find forgiveness.
Leader: Hope in God, you people of God.
People: In God we find steadfast love and redemption.

OR

Leader: God calls all creation to worship!
People: All creation? Even them?
Leader: God calls all creation to worship, even them.
People: God lets anyone come into the fold?
Leader: God yearns for everyone to come into the fold.
People: Thanks be to God! That means I'm welcome as well.

Hymns and Sacred Songs
"O Spirit of the Living God"
found in:
UMH: 539
H82: 531
NCH: 87
LBW: 271

"O Zion, Haste"
found in:
UMH: 573
H82: 539
NNBH: 422
LBW: 397

"God of the Sparrow, God of the Whale"
found in:
UMH: 122
PH: 272
NCH: 592
CH: 725

"God of Many Names"
found in:
UMH: 105
CH: 13

"Arise, Shine Out, Your Light Has Come"
found in:
UMH: 725
PH: 411

"Soften My Heart"
found in:
Renew: 223

"Jesus, Remember Me"
found in:
Renew: 227

Prayer for the Day / Collect
O God who created all that is and called it good: Grant us the

grace to see in all your creatures the spark of your divinity; through Jesus Christ our Savior. Amen.

OR

God, you have created us and called us to be your people. You sent Jesus to gather us together and make us one body, one people. Help us to accept each other as you accept each of us. Amen.

OR

We come together, O God, to acknowledge that you are the one and only true God. It is your will, your reign that is the only sure one. Help us to trust in you and to work with you to bring out the glorious realm you desire to see on earth as in heaven. Amen.

Prayer of Confession
Leader: Let us confess to God and before one another our sins and especially how we let ourselves judge others as being less worthy than ourselves.
People: We confess to you, O God, and before one another that we have sinned. We have failed to be your people. We have failed to follow Jesus. We have called ourselves by his name but we do not side with the untouchables, the unlovely, the unwanted as he did. We are quick to see the sins of others and slow to see our own. Forgive us and empower us with your Spirit to follow Jesus more closely and to love the unlovable as he does. Amen.
Leader: God loves us even when fail to love. God claims us and invites us to become more and more like Jesus, reflecting the love and grace of God.

Prayers of the People (and the Lord's Prayer)

We worship and adore you, O God, for you are the One who created all that is and pronounced it good. You created in great diversity and we are only now beginning to get a glimpse of some of the splendor of your creation both in the far reaches of space and in the subatomic structures within. You reject none of your creation but love each part as dearly as if it were the whole.

(The following paragraph may be used if a separate prayer of confession has not been used.)

We confess to you, O God, and before one another that we have sinned. We have failed to be your people. We have failed to follow Jesus. We have called ourselves by his name but we do not side with the untouchables, the unlovely, the unwanted as he did. We are quick to see the sins of others and slow to see our own. Forgive us and empower us with your Spirit to follow Jesus more closely and to love the unlovable as he does.

We give you thanks for the wonders of creation and for the joy of being a part of such a splendid enterprise. You have given us every good and perfect gift that we need or could desire. You call us good and accept us as your children even when we look like offspring of a lesser, darker power.

(Other thanksgivings may be offered.)

We pray for your creation and all your creatures. We ask you to help us unite together for the common good. Help us to see creation the way you would see it become and then to work for that vision.

(Other intercessions may be offered.)

All these things we ask in the name of our Savior Jesus Christ who taught us to pray together saying:

Our Father... Amen.

(Or if the Lord's Prayer is not used at this point in the service)
All this we ask in the name of the Blessed and Holy Trinity. Amen.

Proper 9
Pentecost 6
Ordinary Time 14

2 Samuel 5:1-5, 9-10
2 Corinthians 12:2-10
Mark 6:1-13

Call to Worship
Leader: Great is God and greatly to be praised.
People: God's holy mountain is the joy of all the earth.
Leader: We think upon God's steadfast love.
People: God's name, like God's praise, reaches the ends of the earth.
Leader: Say to the next generation that this is our God.
People: God will be our guide forever.

OR

Leader: God calls us into the divine presence.
People: We come with joy to worship.
Leader: God calls us to change our minds and our lives.
People: God wants us to change?
Leader: God wants us to change in order to live joyous lives.
People: We trust in God — enough even to change.

Hymns and Sacred Songs
"It's Me, It's Me, O Lord"
found in:
UMH: 352
NNBH: 496
CH: 579

"I Surrender All"
found in:
UMH: 354
AAHH: 396
NNBH: 198

"Dear Lord and Father of Mankind"
found in:
UMH: 358
H82: 652/653
PH: 345
NCH: 502
CH: 594
LBW: 506

"This Is a Day of New Beginnings"
found in:
UMH: 383
NCH: 417
CH: 518

"O Come and Dwell in Me"
found in:
UMH: 388

"Make Me a Captive, Lord"
found in:
UMH: 421
PH: 378

"This Is My Song" (words by Lloyd Stone and Georgia Harkness)
(This is a wonderful hymn to use on patriotic occasions. It allows us to express our patriotism in the context of our faith and in unity with folks of all nations.)
found in:

UMH: 437
NCH: 591
CH: 722

Prayer for the Day / Collect

O God who created us so that we could live in communion with you: Grant us the faith in you to trust that you only invite us to change for our own good; through Jesus Christ our Savior. Amen.

OR

We come to not only worship you, God, but also to receive our marching orders for the week. Where is it you would have us go? What is it that we should do and say? What do we need to change in our lives so that others might know of your love? Open our hearts that we might hear your gracious answers. Amen.

Prayer of Confession

Leader: Let us confess to God and before one another our sins and especially our reluctance to change — even for God.

People: We confess to you, O God, and before our sisters and brothers gathered that we have sinned. We have sinned in what we have done and in what we have left undone. We have sinned in our obstinately clinging to our own ideas of how we need to live our lives. We have failed to consult you and to open our hearts and lives to your loving gaze. We fear that we are not right but we hide from the only thing that can make us right — our repentance. Forgive us and heal us. Give us such faith in you that we will be honest with you and ourselves about the things that need changed in our lives. Help us to clear the two-by-four that is in our eye so that we can help

others remove the dust fleck in theirs. Amen.
Leader: God does love us and desires nothing but our own good. God desires us to have life and to have it abundantly and joyfully. God's desire for us to change is a sure sign of God's love for us. God will not leave us alone in our brokenness.

Prayers of the People (and the Lord's Prayer)
We worship and adore you, O God, because it was out of love and longing that you created us. You did not create us as slaves but as dear children, made in your own image and filled with your own Spirit.

(The following paragraph may be used if a separate prayer of confession has not been used.)
We confess to you, O God, and before our sisters and brothers gathered that we have sinned. We have sinned in what we have done and in what we have left undone. We have sinned in our obstinately clinging to our own ideas of how we need to live our lives. We have failed to consult you and to open our hearts and lives to your loving gaze. We fear that we are not right but we hide from the only thing that can make us right — our repentance. Forgive us and heal us. Give us such faith in you that we will be honest with you and ourselves about the things that need changed in our lives. Help us to clear the two-by-four that is in our eye so that we can help others remove the dust fleck in theirs.

We give you thanks for all the ways that you show your love for us and all creation, even when you ask us to change.

(Other thanksgivings may be offered.)
You know our frame is that but dust. Fill us once again with the power of your Spirit that we may go from glory to glory as we are changed into your likeness.

(Other intercessions may be offered.)
All these things we ask in the name of our Savior Jesus Christ
who taught us to pray together saying:
Our Father... Amen.

(Or if the Lord's Prayer is not used at this point in the service)
All this we ask in the name of the blessed and Holy Trinity.
Amen.

Proper 10
Pentecost 7
Ordinary Time 15

2 Samuel 6:1-5, 12b-19
Ephesians 1:3-14
Mark 6:14-29

Call to Worship
Leader: The earth is God's and all that is in it;
People: the world and all who live therein.
Leader: For God founded it upon the seas,
People: and established it upon the rivers.
Leader: Lift up your heads and open your gates
People: that God the glorious One may enter.

OR

Leader: God calls us to be together.
People: We come to join with our God.
Leader: God calls us to be together with each other too.
People: We come to join our brothers and sisters in this place.
Leader: God calls us together with all God's children.
People: All God's children are our sisters and brothers.

Hymns and Sacred Songs
"Help Us to Accept Each Other"
found in:
UMH: 560
PH: 538
NCH: 388
CH: 487

"Jesus, United by Thy Grace"
found in:
UMH: 561

"Blest Be the Dear United Love"
found in:
UMH: 566

"In Christ There Is No East or West"
found in:
UMH: 548
H82: 529
PH: 439/440
AAHH: 398/399
NNBH: 299
NCH: 394/395
CH: 687
LBW: 259

"We Are the Church"
found in:
UMH: 558

Prayer for the Day / Collect
O God, who is community in your own divine self and who created us to be in communion with you and each other: Grant us the grace to see your great love for all of us so that we may gladly care for one another; through Jesus Christ our Savior. Amen.

OR

Come into our presence and receive our praise and worship, O God. Hear the love of your children and help us to comprehend the glorious community you are creating for us. Amen.

Prayer of Confession
Leader: Let us confess to God and before one another our sins and especially our quickness to forget that God calls us into community with all God's children.
People: We confess to you, O God, and before one another that we have failed to live into the fullness of your image. We have thought of your love in terms of what it means for us and have failed to understand that it is for others as well. We have tried to be in communion with you while we have excluded others from our love and care. Forgive us and so fill us with your Spirit that we desire to love others as much as we desire to love you. Amen.
Leader: God loves us all as children chosen for righteousness and grants us forgives and grace to live as community.

Prayers of the People (and the Lord's Prayer)
We worship and adore you, O God, for you are the perfect mystery of community. We call you the Three in One and though we don't understand all that means, we know it is wondrous and awesome.

(The following paragraph may be used if a separate prayer of confession has not been used.)
We confess to you, O God, and before one another that we have failed to live into the fullness of your image. We have thought of your love in terms of what it means for us and have failed to understand that it is for others as well. We have tried to be in communion with you while we have excluded others from our love and care. Forgive us and so fill us with your Spirit that we desire to love others as much as we desire to love you.

We thank you for Jesus, who taught us what it means to be in union with you and showed us what it means for us to be in union with each other. We thank you for the ways he revealed how even the lowliest are central to your love.

(Other thanksgivings may be offered.)
We offer to your caring heart the hurts of this world as we see it in those we know and as we are aware of it in those we do not know. We pray for those who have no one else to pray for them. We pray for ourselves that we may be more aware of our connection with all your children.

(Other intercessions may be offered.)
All these things we ask in the name of our Savior Jesus Christ who taught us to pray together saying:
Our Father... Amen.

(Or if the Lord's Prayer is not used at this point in the service)
All this we ask in the name of the Blessed and Holy Trinity. Amen.

Proper 11
Pentecost 8
Ordinary Time 16

2 Samuel 7:1-14a
Ephesians 2:11-22
Mark 6:30-34, 53-56

Call to Worship
Leader: Come, let us worship the God who breaks down the walls.
People: We come to worship the One who brings us together.
Leader: God is great and greatly to be praised.
People: There is no division between heaven and earth.
Leader: There is no division between God's earth creatures.
People: Praise be to God who makes us one in Christ.

Hymns and Sacred Songs
"From All that Dwell Below the Skies"
found in:
UMH. 101
H82: 380
PH: 229
NCH: 27
CH: 49
LBW: 550

"God, Who Stretched the Spangled Heavens"
found in:
UMH: 150
H82: 580
PH: 268

NCH: 556
CH: 651
LBW: 463

"Jesu, Jesu"
found in:
UMH: 432
H82: 602
PH: 367
NCH: 498
CH: 600

"*Cuando El Pobre*" ("When the Poor Ones")
found in:
UMH: 434
PH: 407
CH: 662

"What Does the Lord Require?"
found in:
UMH: 441
H82: 605
PH: 505
CH: 659

"Our Parent, by Whose Name"
found in:
UMH: 447
LBW: 357

"The Trees of the Field"
found in:
Renew: 302

"Bind Us Together"
found in:
Renew: 292

Prayer for the Day / Collect

O God who is truly one and yet in communion: Grant us the faith to trust that you accept us into yourself so that we can accept others into our midst; through Jesus Christ our Savior. Amen.

OR

We come to worship because you have invited us, great God of creation. You created all that is to be with you. You invite us into your presence and enable us to live in peace with one another. Help us to praise you and to live in your unity. Amen.

Prayer of Confession

Leader: Let us confess to God and before one another our sins and especially the walls we allow to separate us from one another.

People: We confess to you, O God, and before one another that we have sinned and fallen short of the glory you have in mind for us. We have allowed walls of our own creating to separate us from those you created to be our sisters and brothers. We have made up standards whereby we elevate ourselves and denigrate others. In doing this, we have separated us from your own true self, for you are love eternal and unconditional. Forgive us our sinful, willful ways and call us back to you and to communion with all your people. Amen.

Leader: God loves all creation and the earth creatures who were made in the divine image. God delights to have us return and rejoices when we live in harmony with one another.

221

Know that God forgives you and invites you to make amends of your life and to live fully in God's love.

Prayers of the People (and the Lord's Prayer)

We praise you and adore you, O God who created us and all our sisters and brothers. We praise you for breathing into us your own life at our creation and each time we return to you.

(The following paragraph may be used if a separate prayer of confession has not been used.)

We confess to you, O God, and before one another that we have sinned and fallen short of the glory you have in mind for us. We have allowed walls of our own creating to separate us from those you created to be our sisters and brothers. We have made up standards whereby we elevate ourselves and denigrate others. In doing this, we have separated us from your own true self, for you are love eternal and unconditional. Forgive us our sinful, willful ways and call us back to you and to communion with all your people.

We give you thanks for the diversity of creation and especially the diversity within the family of humanity. Your image is expressed in so many glorious and beautiful ways.

(Other thanksgivings may be offered.)

We pray for ourselves and for each other in our brokenness. Help us to tear down the walls that divide us. Help us to work for justice on behalf of those who are oppressed and denied the full benefits of being your children.

(Other intercessions may be offered.)

All these things we ask in the name of our Savior Jesus Christ who taught us to pray together saying:
Our Father... Amen.

(Or if the Lord's Prayer is not used at this point in the service)
All this we ask in the name of the Blessed and Holy Trinity.
Amen.

Proper 12
Pentecost 9
Ordinary Time 17

2 Samuel 11:1-15
Ephesians 3:14-21
John 6:1-21

Call to Worship
Leader: Fools say there is no God.
People: All are corrupt.
Leader: God looks for wise people.
People: God looks but finds none.
Leader: When people discover it is God who saves
People: then all will rejoice and be glad.

OR

Leader: Come, let us worship that God who is in all and through all.
People: We praise the God who is closer to us than our own breath.
Leader: God breathed divine life into us at creation.
People: It is God's presence in us that makes us human.
Leader: Let us celebrate the divine that empowers us.
People: Let us use that power for the good of all creation.

Hymns and Sacred Songs
"Maker, in Whom We Live"
found in:
UMH: 88

"How Great Thou Art"
found in:
UMH: 77
PII: 467
AAHH: 148
NNBH: 43
CH: 33
LBW: 532

"All Creatures of Our God and King"
found in:
UMH: 62
H82: 400
PH: 455
AAHH: 147
NNBH: 33
NCH: 17
CH: 22
LBW: 527

"Many Gifts, One Spirit"
found in:
UMH: 114
NCH: 177

"God of the Sparrow, God of the Whale"
found in:
UMH: 122
PH: 272
CH: 70

"Praise to the Lord, the Almighty"
found in:
UMH: 139
H82: 390

AAHH: 117
NNBH: 2
NCH: 22
CH: 25

"O Come and Dwell in Me"
found in:
UMH: 388

"Breathe on Me, Breath of God"
found in:
UMH: 420
H82: 508
PH: 316
AAHH: 317
NNBH: 126
NCH: 292
CH: 254
LBW: 488

"Be Not Afraid"
found in:
Renew: 243

"Shine, Jesus, Shine"
found in:
Renew: 247

Prayer for the Day / Collect

O God, who created us in your own image and filled us with your own Spirit: Grant us the wisdom to understand that you are a part of us and that nothing good we do is ever done apart from your presence and power; through Jesus Christ our Savior. Amen.

OR

We come and ask for the power of your presence, O God, because apart from you we can do nothing. You are the Spirit that enlivens us and empowers us to become the creatures you formed us to be. Renew your Spirit within us that we may do the good works you created us to do. Amen.

Prayer of Confession

Leader: Let us confess to God and before one another our sins and especially our self-sufficient disregard for God.

People: We confess to you, O God, and before one another that we have sinned before you, against one another, and against our very selves. We have forgotten who we are and how we were created. We have forgotten that it was only when your breath, your Spirit, your life entered us that we became human. We have acted as if we are able to achieve great things without you. We have taken the credit for accomplishments that have been your doing. Forgive us and grant us the grace to rejoice in all that you do in, for, and through us. Amen.

Leader: God delights in granting us the ability to do great things. Rejoice in God's generosity and allow God to do wondrous things through you.

Prayers of the People (and the Lord's Prayer)

We worship and adore you for your greatness and for your great love. In love and grace you created us and all that exists.

(The following paragraph may be used if a separate prayer of confession has not been used.)

We confess to you, O God, and before one another that we have sinned before you, against one another, and against our very selves. We have forgotten who we are and how we were

227

created. We have forgotten that it was only when your breath, your Spirit, your life entered us that we became human. We have acted as if we are able to achieve great things without you. We have taken the credit for accomplishments that have been your doing. Forgive us and grant us the grace to rejoice in all that you do in, for, and through us.

We thank you for the gifts you have offered us. We thank you for the abilities that seem to be a part of our makeup and for those skills we have been able to acquire. You have been generous and kind to us.

(Other thanksgivings may be offered.)
We offer to your love and grace the hurts and cares of this world. As you move among your creation offering salvation, help us to use the abilities, skills, and power you have given us to be part of your saving work.

(Other intercessions may be offered.)
All these things we ask in the name of our Savior Jesus Christ who taught us to pray together saying:
Our Father... Amen.

(Or if the Lord's Prayer is not used at this point in the service)
All this we ask in the name of the Blessed and Holy Trinity. Amen.

Proper 13
Pentecost 10
Ordinary Time 18

2 Samuel 11:26—12:13a
Ephesians 4:1-16
John 6:24-35

Call to Worship
Leader: Have mercy on us, O God,
People: according to your steadfast love.
Leader: Blot out our transgressions
People: according to your abundant mercy.
Leader: Wash us thoroughly from our iniquity
People: and cleanse us from our sin.

OR

Leader: Let us come into the presence of our God.
People: But we are sinful people.
Leader: God knows that and invites us to confess.
People: But we don't want to own up to our sins.
Leader: Confession is the only way to leave them behind.
People: With trust in God, we will confess the state of our lives.
Leader: When we are honest with ourselves and God,
People: we find freedom and joy in living.

Hymns and Sacred Songs
"Grace Greater than Our Sin"
found in:
UMH: 365

"Dear Lord and Father of Mankind"
found in:
UMH: 358
H82: 652/653
PH: 345
NCH: 502
CH: 594
LBW: 506

"*Pues Si Vivimos*" ("When We Are Living")
found in:
UMH: 356
PH: 400
NCH: 499
CH: 536

"Nothing Between"
found in:
UMH: 373
AAHH: 397
NNBH: 307

"Amazing Grace"
found in:
UMH: 378
H82: 671
PH: 280
AAHH: 271/272
NNBH: 161/162
NCH: 547/548
CH: 246
LBW: 488
Renew: 189

"Forgive Our Sins as We Forgive"
found in:
UMH: 390
H82: 674
PH: 347
LBW: 307
Renew: 184

"Sanctuary"
found in:
CCB: 87
Renew: 185

"Change My Heart, O God"
found in:
CCB: 56

Prayer for the Day / Collect

O God who knows us better than we know ourselves: Grant us the faith we need to trust that you love us and claim us in spite of who we have been; through Jesus Christ our Savior. Amen.

OR

We come to worship you our Creator and Redeemer. We know that we have failed in living fully into your image and yet we come in faith to seek forgiveness and a new start in serving you and others. Amen.

Prayer of Confession

Leader: Let us confess to God and before one another our sins and especially our reticence to confess!

People: We come in reluctance to own up to our own failures and sins. We want to hide them from you, from others, and from ourselves. Yet we know the way to wholeness and holiness must pass through confession. So we confess to you and before our sisters and brothers that we are sinners. We have failed to do the good you have asked us to do, and we have failed to avoid the evil that you have warned us against. Hear us as we name our sins to you and to ourselves. *(time for silent confession)* Forgive us and empower us with your Spirit to move forward in our life in Christ and in our openness about who we are. Amen.

Leader: God knows us and loves us. God remembers that we are but dust. God also remembers that we are filled with the divine life and are precious in God's sight. Live in the truth of who you are so that you can truly become the one who God created you to be.

Prayers of the People (and the Lord's Prayer)

We come to worship and adore you, our God and our guide. You created us out of the dust of the earth and have filled us with your own life. You have created us to be in relationship with you and you open your own life to us.

(The following paragraph may be used if a separate prayer of confession has not been used.)

We come in reluctance to own up to our own failures and sins. We want to hide them from you, from others, and from ourselves. Yet we know the way to wholeness and holiness must pass through confession. So we confess to you and before our sisters and brothers that we are sinners. We have failed to do the good you have asked us to do, and we have failed to avoid the evil that you have warned us against. Hear us as we name our sins to you and to ourselves. *(time for silent confession)* Forgive us and empower us with your Spirit to move forward in our life in Christ and in our openness about who we are.

We give you thanks for all the ways you have shown your love for us. We thank you for the joy of being forgiven and the wonder of discovering that we don't have to hide from you or from ourselves. We are imperfect but we are loved.

(Other thanksgivings may be offered.)
We pray for one another in our needs. We pray that your Spirit would empower us to be less critical and judgmental of others as we find you are not critical or judgmental of us. Help us to be more like you caring for those we see who are in need. Help us to share the goods of this world and the love of heaven with them all.

(Other intercessions may be offered.)
All these things we ask in the name of our Savior Jesus Christ who taught us to pray together saying:
Our Father... Amen.

(Or if the Lord's Prayer is not used at this point in the service)
All this we ask in the name of the Blessed and Holy Trinity. Amen.

Proper 14
Pentecost 11
Ordinary Time 19

2 Samuel 18:5-9, 15, 31-33
Ephesians 4:25—5:2
John 6:34, 41-51

Call to Worship
Leader: Hear our voice, O God.
People: Let your ears be attentive to our supplications.
Leader: If you should mark iniquities, who could stand?
People: Then we find forgiveness in you.
Leader: Hope in God.
People: In God we find steadfast love and redemption.

OR

Leader: Let us come and worship the God who is truth.
People: We come to praise the One in whom there is no falseness.
Leader: God invites us to reflect the divine image.
People: In truth we open our lives to God and one another.
Leader: Let us praise the One who knows us and loves us.
People: Let us commit ourselves to the truth.

Hymns and Sacred Songs
"God, Whose Love Is Reigning O'er Us"
found in:
UMH: 100

"How Can We Name a Love?"
found in:
UMH: 111

"Your Love, O God"
found in:
UMH: 120
CH: 71

"All My Hope Is Firmly Grounded"
found in:
UMH: 132
H82: 665
NCH: 408
CH: 88

"Help Us Accept Each Other"
found in:
UMH: 560
PH: 358
NCH: 388
CH: 487

"Forgive Our Sins as We Forgive"
found in:
UMH: 390
H82: 674
PH: 347
LBW: 307
Renew: 184

"Freely, Freely"
found in:
UMH: 389
Renew: 192

"Great Is the Lord"
found in:
CCB: 65
Renew: 22

"I Call You Faithful"
found in:
CCB: 70

Prayer for the Day / Collect
O God who is true compassion: Grant us the grace to not only accept forgiveness for ourselves but also to offer it to others; through Jesus Christ our Savior. Amen.

OR

We come into your presence, gracious God, at your invitation. You invite sinners to come and find forgiveness. You invite your forgiven people to share that forgiveness with others. Help us to not only receive but also to share with others your loving forgiveness. Amen.

Prayer of Confession
Leader: Let us confess to God and before one another our sins and especially our tendency to receive forgiveness for ourselves more easily than we grant it to others.
People: We confess to you, O God, and before one another that we have sinned. We have failed to be your obedient people. We have not loved you with our whole hearts and we have not loved others as we love ourselves. We are quick to receive your forgiveness even though we know we will be back next week seeking it again for the same sins. Yet we are loathe to offer forgiveness to others until we are satisfied that they have paid sufficiently for the hurt they have given us. We are quick to speak the

"truth" about others but slow to speak it about ourselves. Forgive us our hypocritical ways and grant that we might know the depth of your forgiveness as we offer it to others. Amen.

Leader: God delights in our relationship and gladly forgives us so that we can open ourselves completely to God's presence. God also delights in our relationship with others as we forgive one another. May the power of the Spirit enable us all to forgive as we have been forgiven.

Prayers of the People (and the Lord's Prayer)

We worship and adore you, O God, for you are the One who is always true. Your word is sure and your promises everlasting.

(The following paragraph may be used if a separate prayer of confession has not been used.)

We confess to you, O God, and before one another that we have sinned. We have failed to be your obedient people. We have not loved you with our whole hearts and we have not loved others as we love ourselves. We are quick to receive your forgiveness even though we know we will be back next week seeking it again for the same sins. Yet we are loathe to offer forgiveness to others until we are satisfied that they have paid sufficiently for the hurt they have given us. We are quick to speak the "truth" about others but slow to speak it about ourselves. Forgive us our hypocritical ways and grant that we might know the depth of your forgiveness as we offer it to others.

We give you thanks for all your kindness toward us. We thank you that you love us even though you know the truth of our lives. We thank you that you are the one whose relationship with us is assured forever.

(Other thanksgivings may be offered.)

We know that there is much deceit in this world and many find themselves harmed by the lies they hear and the lies they tell. We pray that we may be a community where truth prevails so that we might be set free.

(Other intercessions may be offered.)
All these things we ask in the name of our Savior Jesus Christ who taught us to pray together saying:
Our Father... Amen.

(Or if the Lord's Prayer is not used at this point in the service)
All this we ask in the name of the Blessed and Holy Trinity. Amen.

Proper 15
Pentecost 12
Ordinary Time 20

1 Kings 2:10-12; 3:3-14
Ephesians 5:15-20
John 6:51-58

Call to Worship
Leader: Let us praise God together!
People: We will give thanks to God with our whole heart.
Leader: Great are the works of God.
People: Those who delight in them, study them.
Leader: God has sent redemption to the people.
People: God's covenant is forever. Awesome is God's name.

OR

Leader: Let us praise the God of wisdom.
People: Praise be to the One who understands all things.
Leader: God invites us to be wise as well.
People: Let us enter into the holy wisdom of God.
Leader: This wisdom is about more than knowing.
People: We will study and we will practice God's wisdom.

Hymns and Sacred Songs
"From All that Dwell Below the Skies"
found in:

UMH: 101
H82: 380
PH: 229
NCH: 27
CH: 49
LBW: 550

"Immortal, Invisible, God Only Wise"
found in:
UMH: 103
H82: 423
PH: 263
NCH: 1
CH: 66
LBW: 523
Renew: 46

"Praise to the Lord, the Almighty"
found in:
UMH: 139
H82: 390
AAHH: 117
NNBH: 2
NCH: 22
CH: 25
Renew: 57

"I Sing the Almighty Power of God"
found in:
UMH: 152
H82: 398
PH: 288
NCH: 12
Renew: 54

"Come, Thou Fount of Every Blessing"
found in:
UMH: 400
H82: 686
PH: 356
AAHH: 175
NNBH: 166
NCH: 459
CH: 16
LBW: 499

"Let There Be Peace on Earth"
found in:
UMH: 431
CH: 677

"Be Thou My Vision"
found in:
UMH: 451
H82: 488
PH: 339
NCH: 451
CH: 595
Renew: 151

"Awesome God"
found in:
CCB: 17
Renew: 245

"Glorify Thy Name"
found in:
CCB: 8
Renew: 37

"Open Our Eyes, Lord"
found in:
CCB: 77
Renew: 91

Prayer for the Day / Collect

O God who is wisdom: Grant us the grace to choose your wise way of living that we may enjoy your eternal life always; through Jesus Christ our Savior. Amen.

OR

We come to worship you, our God, because you know all things in heaven and on earth. There is nothing hidden from you and you know the way that leads to eternal life. Grant us the grace to accept your invitation to live by your wisdom that we may also share your life. Amen.

Prayer of Confession

Leader: Let us confess to God and before one another our sins and especially the folly of our lives.

People: We confess to you, O God, and before one another that we have sinned. You have shown us the way to life that is full, abundant, and eternal and yet we have chosen to follow our own paths. You have pointed out to us the things that lead to death and the things that lead to life. We have chosen death over and over again. Forgive us our foolish ways and call us back once more to your path of wisdom and life. Amen.

Leader: The God of wisdom is also the God of compassion. God forgives us and invites us to once again enter the path that leads to life.

Prayers of the People (and the Lord's Prayer)

We worship and adore you, O God, because you are wise beyond our understanding. You know the secrets of the universe and the secrets of our hearts. You see the truth about death and about life and the way to enter into each.

(The following paragraph may be used if a separate prayer of confession has not been used.)

We confess to you, O God, and before one another that we have sinned. You have shown us the way to life that is full, abundant, and eternal and yet we have chosen to follow our own paths. You have pointed out to us the things that lead to death and the things that lead to life. We have chosen death over and over again. Forgive us our foolish ways and call us back once more to your path of wisdom and life.

We give you thanks for all the ways you share your wisdom with us from the knowledge you share about the wonders of creation and the ways you enable us to unlock these mysteries, to the more important knowledge about the nature of true life. We thank you for inviting us to share your wisdom and your eternal life.

(Other thanksgivings may be offered.)

We offer up to you those who find themselves on the wrong path. They haven't meant to choose death. Some have been seduced by the world and some are on the path to destruction because we have failed to share the good news with them. Bless them and call them back to life. Enable us by the power of your Spirit to help them find their way.

(Other intercessions may be offered.)

All these things we ask in the name of our Savior Jesus Christ who taught us to pray together saying:
Our Father... Amen.

(Or if the Lord's Prayer is not used at this point in the service)
All this we ask in the name of the Blessed and Holy Trinity.
Amen.

Proper 16
Pentecost 13
Ordinary Time 21

1 Kings 8:(1, 6, 10-11) 22-30, 41-43
Ephesians 6:10-20
John 6:56-69

Call to Worship
Leader: How lovely is your dwelling place, O God!
People: My soul longs, it faints, for God's courts.
Leader: My heart and my flesh sing for joy to God.
People: Even the birds of the air find a home with God.
Leader: Hear the plea of your servant and of your people.
People: Hear our voice and forgive us, O God.

OR

Leader: God calls us to worship and to service.
People: We know how to worship God but God's service is hard.
Leader: God asks us to take on a new agenda, God's priorities.
People: We struggle to know what these are.
Leader: God honors your struggle if it is honest.
People: In honesty we will confront the world as God's children.

Hymns and Sacred Songs
"This Is My Father's World"
found in:
UMH: 144
H82: 651

PH: 293
AAHH: 149
NNBH: 41
CH: 59
LBW: 554

"I Sing the Almighty Power of God"
found in:
UMH: 152
H82: 398
PH: 288
NCH: 12

"God of the Ages"
found in:
UMH: 698
PH: 262
NCH: 592

"Where Cross the Crowded Ways of Life"
found in:
UMH: 427
H82: 609
PH: 408
NCH: 543
CH: 665
LBW: 429

"People Need the Lord"
found in:
CCB: 52

Prayer for the Day / Collect
O God who sees the world as it was created to be: Grant us
the wisdom to see the ways in which we can help move the

world toward your goal and to see the methods that will do this with integrity; through Jesus Christ our Savior. Amen.

OR

We come to praise you, our God, and hear if you have a word for us today. We know that you love the world and seek its salvation. Help us to understand how we can be part of your great works of salvation in this time and place. Amen.

Prayer of Confession
Leader: Let us confess to God and before one another our sins and especially the ways in which we insert our own goals into our religious life and call them God's goals.
People: We confess to you, O God, and before one another that we are often blinded by our own goals and do not see that your goals may be different from ours. We see only the ways in which we would solve the issue of the day and we fail to ask you how you desire things to be handled. Forgive us and empower us with your Spirit so that we may truly be your children and disciples of your Son, Jesus the Christ. Amen.
Leader: God is about the work of salvation and wishes to draw us into that great work. First, God draws us through repentance into God's great reign and then God sends us out to complete that work in all creation. Through the power and grace of God, we are forgiven.

Prayers of the People (and the Lord's Prayer)
We worship and praise your name, O God, because you are the wisdom before all the ages. Before there existed anything, you knew how you wanted the creation to be. You saw us in the splendor of your own intentions.

(The following paragraph may be used if a separate prayer of confession has not been used.)
We confess to you, O God, and before one another that we are often blinded by our own goals and do not see that your goals may be different from ours. We see only the ways in which we would solve the issue of the day and we fail to ask you how you desire things to be handled. Forgive us and empower us with your Spirit so that we may truly be your children and disciples of your Son, Jesus the Christ.

We give you thanks for the ways in which you have brought your intentions into being. We thank you for those who have listened carefully to your voice and have acted in the power of your Spirit to bring salvation more fully into being. We thank you for the ways in which your reign has been made known to us.

(Other thanksgivings may be offered.)
We pray for this creation, which needs so desperately to know your reign. We pray for ourselves and your entire church, which needs to know your will and obedience to your reign.

(Other intercessions may be offered.)
All these things we ask in the name of our Savior Jesus Christ who taught us to pray together saying:
Our Father... Amen.

(Or if the Lord's Prayer is not used at this point in the service)
All this we ask in the name of the Blessed and Holy Trinity. Amen.

Proper 17
Pentecost 14
Ordinary 22

Song of Solomon 2:8-13
James 1:17-27
Mark 7:1-8, 14-15, 21-23

Call to Worship
Leader: God's throne endures forever and ever.
People: God's scepter is a scepter of equity.
Leader: When we love righteousness and hate wickedness,
People: then God anoints us with the oil of gladness.
Leader: Then we smell the sweetness of God
People: and our ears are pleased with pleasant sounds.

OR

Leader: God calls us to this time of worship.
People: We come with songs and words of praise.
Leader: The worship of God is also quietness and listening.
People: We will tune our ears to what God has to say to us.
Leader: Sometimes God speaks through the mouths of others.
People: We will listen to one another as we listen to God.

Hymns and Sacred Songs
"Now Thank We All Our God"
found in:
UMH: 102
H82: 396/397
PH: 557

NNBH: 330
NCH: 419
CH: 715
LBW: 533/534

"Dear Lord, Lead Me Day by Day"
found in:
UMH: 411

"Blest Be the Tie that Binds"
found in:
UMH: 557
PH: 438
AAHH: 341
NNBH: 298
NCH: 393
CH: 433
LBW: 370

"Jesus, Stand Among Us" (words and music by Graham Kendrick)
Renew: 17

Prayer for the Day / Collect
O God who walked with our first parents in the cool of the day: Grant us the wisdom to see that respectful listening is part of living in your image; through Jesus Christ our Savior. Amen.

OR

O God, we have come to worship you and to listen to you. As you open your heart to us, let us open our heart to you. Help us to recognize that you also speak to us through one another. Amen.

Prayer of Confession

Leader: Let us confess to God and before one another our sins and especially how we fail to listen to God and to one another.

People: We confess to you, O God, and before one another that we have sinned. Although we have been created with one mouth and two ears, we are sure that it is more important for us to talk than to listen. We think that our telling you what we want is more important than hearing you tell us where to find life. We think it is more important to share our thoughts with others than for their thoughts to be shared with us. We are truly self-centered people. Forgive us such foolishness and open our ears by the power of your Spirit that we might truly hear you and our sisters and brothers. Amen.

Leader: God loves and longs to listen to us and to speak to us. God forgives us and empowers us to listen.

Prayers of the People (and the Lord's Prayer)

Holy and glory are you, O God, for you have created us for yourself. You have longed to be in communion with us and all creation. You listen to the cries of your people and long to hear from them. You desire a loving relationship with each of us and to share our lives.

(The following paragraph may be used if a separate prayer of confession has not been used.)

We confess to you, O God, and before one another that we have sinned. Although we have been created with one mouth and two ears, we are sure that it is more important for us to talk than to listen. We think that our telling you what we want is more important than hearing you tell us where to find life. We think it is more important to share our thoughts with others than for their thoughts to be shared with us. We are truly self-centered people. Forgive us such foolishness and open our ears by the power of your Spirit that we might truly hear you and our sisters and brothers.

We give you thanks for all the good we have received from your hand. You have blessed us with creation and you have blessed us with your own love and presence. Your Spirit dwells within us and among us so that we may find life as we live in you.

(Other thanksgivings may be offered.)
We offer to you the cares and worries of our hearts. In confidence of your love for us and for all your people, we offer to you those who suffer in body, mind, or spirit. We pray for those who have not yet heard your voice of love and acceptance. We pray for ourselves that we may be part of your loving, listening presence.

(Other intercessions may be offered.)
All these things we ask in the name of our Savior Jesus Christ who taught us to pray together saying:
Our Father... Amen.

(Or if the Lord's Prayer is not used at this point in the service)
All this we ask in the name of the Blessed and Holy Trinity. Amen.

Proper 18
Pentecost 15
Ordinary Time 23

Proverbs 22:1-2, 8-9, 22-23
James 2:1-10 (11-13) 14-17
Mark 7:24-37

Call to Worship
Leader: Those who trust in God are like Mount Zion,
People: they cannot be moved.
Leader: As the mountains surround Jerusalem,
People: God surrounds us now and forever.
Leader: Do not let the scepter of wickedness dwell among
us
**People: so that we will not stretch out our hands and do
wrong.**

OR

Leader: God created us all.
People: God has created the rich and poor alike.
Leader: In Christ we are neither rich nor poor.
People: In Christ we are all sisters and brothers.
Leader: All are our neighbors.
**People: We are to love them all as much as we love our-
selves.**

Hymns and Sacred Songs
"*Cuando El Pobre*" ("When the Poor Ones")
found in:
UMH: 434

PH: 407
CH: 662

"What Does the Lord Require?"
found in:
UMH: 441
H82: 605
PH: 405
CH: 659

"Jesu, Jesu"
found in:
UMH: 432
H82: 602
PH: 367
NCH: 498
CH: 600
CCB:66
Renew: 289

"The Gift of Love"
found in:
UMH: 408
AAHH: 522
CH: 526
Renew: 155

"Make Me a Servant"
found in:
CCB: 90

"We Are His Hands"
found in:
CCB: 85

Prayer for the Day / Collect

O God who is the Creator of all your children: Grant us the grace and wisdom to see every person as endowed with your image and Spirit that we may honor them as we honor our Savior; through Jesus Christ our Savior. Amen.

OR

We come to worship you, our Creator, who made us all in your own image. As we offer our praises to you we ask that you would open our hearts not only to your presence but also to the presence of those around us in this place and throughout all the world. Amen.

Prayer of Confession

Leader: Let us confess to God and before one another our sins and especially the ways in which we ignore the needs of those around us.

People: We confess to you, O God, and before one another that we have sinned. We know that we feel more comfortable around those who look and act like us. We are aware that we like to rub elbows with those who have money and power. It makes us feel more important. Forgive us our silliness and by the power of your Spirit call us back to be true disciples of Jesus. Help us to see once again that we are only great when we stoop to help those who need us. Amen.

Leader: God loves us and sees the poverty of our lives even when we have material wealth. God honors our truthful confession about who we are and grants us not only forgiveness but the gracious Spirit to empower us to live as faithful disciples of Jesus.

Prayers of the People (and the Lord's Prayer)

We praise and worship you, our Creator most holy, for the

wonders we see around us. We see the starry heavens and the flora and fauna of this earth. We see your image in the multiplicity of humanity.

(The following paragraph may be used if a separate prayer of confession has not been used.)
We confess to you, O God, and before one another that we have sinned. We know that we feel more comfortable around those who look and act like us. We are aware that we like to rub elbows with those who have money and power. It makes us feel more important. Forgive us our silliness and by the power of your Spirit call us back to be true disciples of Jesus. Help us to see once again that we are only great when we stoop to help those who need us.

We give you thanks for all the blessings of our lives. We thank you for good food we have to eat and the many material things we have access to in this life. We thank you for the abundance of creation and the way in which it provides beyond our needs.

(Other thanksgivings may be offered.)
We pray for those who have been denied the goodness of your creation. There are many who are hungry and far too many starving to death. We have brothers and sisters around the world who are naked and without shelter. Some are without the most basic of needs, not even decent water to drink. Many live in abject poverty, even living in dumps. We pray for them and for ourselves that we may reach out to them in their needs as we would hope to take care of ourselves and as we would desire to take care of you for we know you in them.

(Other intercessions may be offered.)
All these things we ask in the name of our Savior Jesus Christ who taught us to pray together saying:

Our Father... Amen.

(Or if the Lord's Prayer is not used at this point in the service)
All this we ask in the name of the Blessed and Holy Trinity. Amen.

Proper 19
Pentecost 16
Ordinary Time 24

Proverbs 1:20-33
James 3:1-12
Mark 8:27-38

Call to Worship
Leader: The heavens tell the glory of God;
People: the firmament proclaims God's handiwork.
Leader: The law of God is perfect.
People: God's law revives our souls.
Leader: The decrees of God are sure.
People: By them are we made wise.

OR

Leader: God calls us to gather for worship.
People: We come as God's people together.
Leader: God calls us all but also calls each one.
People: God knows our name and draws us near.
Leader: God is the One who gives us our identity.
People: As children of God we know we are loved.

Hymns and Sacred Songs
"I Am Thine, O Lord"
found in:
UMH: 419
AAHH: 387
NNBH: 202
NCH: 455
CH: 601

"Where He Leads Me"
found in:
UMH: 338
AAHH: 550
NNBH: 429
CH: 346

"Blest Be the Tie that Binds"
found in:
UMH: 557
PH: 438
AAHH: 341
NNBH: 298
NCH: 393
CH: 433
LBW: 370

"Christ, from Whom All Blessings Flow"
found in:
UMH: 550

"O How He Loves You and Me!"
found in:
CCB: 38
Renew: 27

"I Am Loved"
found in:
CCB: 80

Prayer for the Day / Collect
O God who created us and has called us by name: Grant us
the grace to know we are of great value because we are loved
by you; through Jesus Christ our Savior. Amen.

OR

God, you have created us and filled us with your own life. No one knows us better than you know us, not even ourselves. In that knowledge you love us and call us your very own children. Help us to always find our identity and worth in you. Amen.

OR

O God who created us to sing your praises: Grant us the grace to use our gift of speech to praise you and bless others that we may truly be your children; through Jesus Christ our Savior. Amen.

Prayer of Confession

Leader: Let us confess to God and before one another our sins especially when we use our speech in ways that are destructive instead of building God's reign.

People: We confess to you, O God, and before one another that we have sinned. We have taken the glorious gift of speech and twisted it into a curse. We have inflamed others by our thoughtless words and have caused others to be hurt by what we have said. We have failed to bless and we have been quick to curse. Forgive us and send your Spirit to quell the fire within that we might truly be your image and your children. Amen.

Leader: God loves us and knows how weak we are. God forgives us and grants us the power of the Spirit to live in the fullness of God's reign.

Prayers of the People (and the Lord's Prayer)

We praise and worship you, O God, for your great glory. You are the giver of all true and perfect gifts.

(The following paragraph may be used if a separate prayer of confession has not been used.)

We confess to you, O God, and before one another that we have sinned. We have taken the glorious gift of speech and twisted it into a curse. We have inflamed others by our thoughtless words and have caused others to be hurt by what we have said. We have failed to bless and we have been quick to curse. Forgive us and send your Spirit to quell the fire within that we might truly be your image and your children.

We give you thanks for the wonderful gifts you have given to us. You have given us eyes to see the beauty around us; ears to hear music, nature, and words of love. You have given us the ability to enjoy the aroma of freshly baked bread and the gift of touch to know we are not alone. You have also given us the ability to speak so that we can praise and worship you.

(Other thanksgivings may be offered.)

We pray for those we have hurt in our thoughtless speech and those we have failed in not giving them a word of hope or encouragement. We pray for those who long to hear a word of love and care. We pray for ourselves as your messengers of hope.

(Other intercessions may be offered.)

All these things we ask in the name of our Savior Jesus Christ who taught us to pray together saying:
Our Father... Amen.

(Or if the Lord's Prayer is not used at this point in the service)

All this we ask in the name of the Blessed and Holy Trinity. Amen.

Proper 20
Pentecost 17
Ordinary Time 25

Proverbs 31:10-31
James 3:13—4:3, 7-8a
Mark 9:30-37

Call to Worship
Leader: Happy are those who do not follow the advice of the wicked;
People: happy are those who do not follow the path of sinners.
Leader: Happy are those who delight in God's law.
People: Happy are those who meditate on God's law day and night.
Leader: In God we grow as trees beside streams of water.
People: In God we find that our ways flourish.

OR

Leader: God calls us together as children.
People: We are God's children and God's family.
Leader: Jesus does not call us to be self-centered and whiny.
People: God calls us to take our place as the lowly servant.
Leader: Jesus sets the example for us.
People: If we would follow Jesus, we must serve all.

Hymns and Sacred Songs
"Make Me a Captive, Lord"
found in:

UMH: 421
PH: 378

"Love Divine, All Loves Excelling"
found in:
UMH: 384
H82: 657
PH: 376
AAHH: 440
NNBH: 65
NCH: 43
CH: 517
LBW: 315
Renew: 196

"*Cuando El Pobre*" ("When the Poor Ones")
found in:
UMH: 434
PH: 407
CH: 662

"Jesu, Jesu"
found in:
UMH: 432
H82: 602
PH: 367
NCH: 498
CH: 600
CCB: 66
Renew: 289

"What Does the Lord Require?"
found in:
UMH: 441
H82: 605

PH: 405
CH: 370

"What Wondrous Love Is This?"
found in:
UMH: 292
H82: 439
PH: 85
NCH: 223
CH: 200
LBW: 385
Renew: 227

"Behold, What Manner of Love"
found in:
CCB: 44

"Live in Charity"
found in:
CCB: 71

"Make Me a Servant"
found in:
CCB: 90

Prayer for the Day / Collect
O God who is great and rules over all and yet comes to us as a servant: Grant us the grace to follow Jesus and to serve others as he has served us; through Jesus Christ our Savior. Amen.

OR

We come into your presence, O God, and offer you our praise and adoration. You are the great One who sits enthroned in high and lofty grandeur. Yet you are also the one who walks with us in the cool of the day and wipes away our tears. Help us to learn from Jesus that we might be more like you. Amen.

Prayer of Confession

Leader: Let us confess to God and before one another our sins and especially the ways in which we try to gain place and stature rather than living lives of service.

People: We confess to you, O God, and before one another that we have sinned. Instead of acting as servants of all and with childlike faith, we have pushed others aside to get the places of honor. We have found our status from the world and not as Jesus' slaves. Forgive us and inspire us once more with your Spirit that we may truly follow Jesus. Amen.

Leader: God loves all the children of the world — even when we act more like children of the devil than children of God. God forgives us and sends us out to serve the world in Jesus' name.

Prayers of the People (and the Lord's Prayer)

We offer to you our praise and worship, O God, and bow our hearts before you. You are the most awesome of the most awesome and sit enthroned above all.

(The following paragraph may be used if a separate prayer of confession has not been used.)

We confess to you, O God, and before one another that we have sinned. Instead of acting as servants of all and with childlike faith, we have pushed others aside to get the places of honor. We have found our status from the world and not as Jesus' slaves. Forgive us and inspire us once more with your Spirit that we may truly follow Jesus.

265

We thank you for your loving presence among and within us. It is with deepest gratitude that we reflect on the way in which you have served us in love and grace. From your creating us to your sending Jesus to call us back into your reign, you have faithfully sought for our good and salvation.

(Other thanksgivings may be offered.)
We offer to you the hurts and cares of the world. We pray for those we will have an opportunity serve this week. May our service be filled with your grace.

(Other intercessions may be offered.)
All these things we ask in the name of our Savior Jesus Christ who taught us to pray together saying:
Our Father... Amen.

(Or if the Lord's Prayer is not used at this point in the service)
All this we ask in the name of the Blessed and Holy Trinity. Amen.

Proper 21
Pentecost 18
Ordinary Time 26

Esther 7:1-6, 9-10; 9:20-22
James 5:13-20
Mark 9:38-50

Call to Worship
Leader: If God were not on our side,
People: we would be like prey swallowed alive.
Leader: We have escaped like a bird from the snare.
People: The snare is broken and we are free.
Leader: Our help is in the name of our God.
People: God is the Creator of heaven and earth.

OR

Leader: God calls all of the children of the earth.
People: God calls in terms that each can hear.
Leader: God speaks in various languages, signs, and voices.
People: God speaks to us in our own heart language.
Leader: God loves us enough to speak so we can hear.
People: Let us share God's love in the same way.

Hymns and Sacred Songs
"God of Many Names"
found in:
UMH: 105
CH: 13

"Many Gifts, One Spirit"
found in:

UMH: 114
NCH: 177

"How Can We Name a Love?"
found in:
UMH: 111

"Source and Sovereign, Rock and Cloud"
found in:
UMH: 113
CH: 12

"God of the Sparrow, God of the Whale"
found in:
UMH: 122
PH: 272
NCH: 32
CH: 70

"*Tu Has Venido a la Orilla*" ("Lord, You Have Come to the Lakeshore")
found in:
UMH: 344
PH: 377
CH: 342

"Open Our Eyes, Lord"
found in:
CCB: 77
Renew: 91

"People Need the Lord"
CCB: 52

Prayer for the Day / Collect

O God who created us and knows us to the deepest recesses of our souls: Grant us the wisdom to share that love in ways that others can perceive clearly and respond to you; through Jesus Christ our Savior. Amen.

OR

You have called us here, O God, so that we might share love with you and one another. In all our differences you have found a way to speak to each of us. Help us to learn to speak to others in ways that they can hear the good news of Jesus. Amen.

Prayer of Confession

Leader: Let us confess to God and before one another our sins and especially the way we insist that others be like us. **People: We confess to you, O God, and before one another that we have sinned. We have made our experiences to be the norm for everyone. We think that our way is the only way. We despair that others use such ways of talking about you. Forgive our selfish ways and help us by the power of your Spirit to open our hearts and minds to the ways in that you may be reaching out to your children. Amen.** Leader: God hears us whenever we try to connect with the divine. God grant us forgiveness and the power and love to reach out to others so they may come to know God better.

Prayers of the People (and the Lord's Prayer)

We praise and worship our Creator God who knows us better than we know ourselves. You know our history and our makeup. You know what opens our hearts and what shuts us down.

(The following paragraph may be used if a separate prayer of confession has not been used.)
We confess to you, O God, and before one another that we have sinned. We have made our experiences to be the norm for everyone. We think that our way is the only way. We despair that others use such ways of talking about you. Forgive our selfish ways and help us by the power of your Spirit to open our hearts and minds to the ways in that you may be reaching out to your children.

With grateful hearts we thank you for all the blessings we have received from you. We thank you for the ways in which your love and grace has been expressed to us so that we have been able to receive it. We thank you for those who were faithful in sharing your love with us.

(Other thanksgivings may be offered.)
We lift up to your caring heart the hurts and needs of our world. We pray that you would empower us to reach out in grace to those around us. Help us to understand the ways in which others can hear you speak through us whether in word or in deed. Help us to be open channels by which you call your children home.

(Other intercessions may be offered.)
All these things we ask in the name of our Savior Jesus Christ who taught us to pray together saying:
Our Father... Amen.

(Or if the Lord's Prayer is not used at this point in the service)
All this we ask in the name of the Blessed and Holy Trinity. Amen.

Proper 22
Pentecost 19
Ordinary Time 27

Job 1:1; 2:1-10
Hebrews 1:1-4; 2:5-12
Mark 10:2-16

Call to Worship
Leader: Prove us, O God, and try us.
People: Test our hearts and our minds,
Leader: for your steadfast love is before us
People: and we walk in faithfulness to you.
Leader: Our feet stand on level ground;
People: in the congregation we will bless you, O God.

OR

Leader: You have called us together, O God.
People: You have called us to this place of worship.
Leader: You have called all your people together.
People: You have called those who worship in other places.
Leader: You have called all people together.
People: You have called those who know you and those who do not.

OR

Leader: You have called us into loving relationship with yourself.
People: You have called us to care for others as ourselves.

Leader: You have called us to watch over one another in love.

People: You have called us to esteem others over ourselves.

Leader: We offer to you our worship, O God.

People: And we offer to others the care you would have for them.

Hymns and Sacred Songs
"Forward Through the Ages"
found in:
UMC: 555
NCH: 377

"Where Charity and Love Prevail"
found in:
UMC: 549
H82: 581
NCH: 396
LBW: 126

"Here, O Lord, Your Servants Gather"
found in:
UMC: 552
PH: 465
CH: 278

"We Are One in Christ Jesus" ("*Somos uno en Cristo*")
found in:
CCB: 43

Prayer for the Day / Collect
O God who created us as one people: Grant us the grace to accept each other in all our diversity and so give honor to

you, our Creator and theirs; through Jesus Christ our Savior. Amen.

OR

O God who created us for relationships: Grant us the grace to give you all of our love and being and to care for others with the same intensity that we care for ourselves; through Jesus Christ our Savior. Amen.

OR

We come to worship you the God of all the people. We offer to you our praise and ask that you would receive it — inadequate as it may be. Help us to see in others the image you placed upon them at their creation. May we witness to your love for the world as we love all. Amen.

Prayer of Confession
Leader: Let us confess to God and before one another our sins and especially the walls we build between ourselves and others.
People: We confess to you, O God, and before one another that we have sinned against you and your children. We have ignored the sacred stories that tell us we are all your children created out of one love. We have forgotten the story of Pentecost where you spoke to a wondrously diverse crowd through Peter's preaching. We have tried to make ourselves look good by making others look bad or at least not as good. Forgive us and so fill us with your Spirit that we can do nothing but love you and all your people. Amen.
Leader: God loves all of God's people — even us. God redeems you so that you can spread God's love for and to all people.

Prayers of the People (and the Lord's Prayer)

We worship and adore you, O God, because you are the first love of all creation. Out of your great heart of love you created us, all of us, to be in a loving relationship with you and with each other. You indeed are love.

(The following paragraph may be used if a separate prayer of confession has not been used.)
We confess to you, O God, and before one another that we have sinned against you and your children. We have ignored the sacred stories that tell us we are all your children created out of one love. We have forgotten the story of Pentecost where you spoke to a wondrously diverse crowd through Peter's preaching. We have tried to make ourselves look good by making others look bad or at least not as good. Forgive us and so fill us with your Spirit that we can do nothing but love you and all your people.

We give you thanks for all the ways in which we have experienced your love. For your love that has come to us through human beings we are grateful. For your love that we have experienced in the wonders of nature or the beauty of art and music, we give you thanks.

(Other thanksgivings may be offered.)
We pray for the needs of your creation. We know that to experience your love is the greatest need of all of us. We ask that all we do and say this week may be a means of grace and love for those who come in contact with us.

(Other intercessions may be offered.)
All these things we ask in the name of our Savior Jesus Christ who taught us to pray together saying:
Our Father... Amen.

(Or if the Lord's Prayer is not used at this point in the service)
All this we ask in the name of the Blessed and Holy Trinity.
Amen.

Proper 23
Pentecost 20
Ordinary Time 28

Job 23:1-9, 16-17
Hebrews 4:12-16
Mark 10:17-31

Call to Worship
Leader: Our God, why have you forsaken us?
People: Why are you so far from helping us?
Leader: We cry by day and you do not answer.
People: We cry by night and get no rest.
Leader: Yet you are holy, enthroned by our praises.
People: In you our ancestors trusted and were delivered.

OR

Leader: Jesus calls us to hear the good news.
People: We are ready to hear the good news.
Leader: Jesus comes to free us from our possessions.
People: But we like our stuff.
Leader: Jesus invites us to own stuff and not be owned by it.
People: That is freedom, indeed!

Hymns and Sacred Songs
"Morning Has Broken"
found in:
UMH: 145
H82: 8

PH: 469
CH: 53

"Many and Great, O God"
found in:
UMH: 148
H82: 385
PH: 267
NCH: 3
CH: 58

"All Things Bright and Beautiful"
found in:
UMH: 147
H82: 405
PH: 267
NCH: 31
CH: 61

"*Cantemos al Senor*" ("Let's Sing Unto the Lord")
found in:
UMH: 149
NCH: 39
CH: 60
Renew: 11

"*Cuando el Pobre*" ("When the Poor Ones")
found in:
UMH: 434
PH: 407
CH: 662

"O God Who Shaped Creation"
found in:
UMH: 443

"For the Healing of the Nations"
found in:
UMH: 428
NCH: 576
CH: 668

"All I Need Is You"
found in:
CCB: 100

"As the Deer"
found in:
CCB:83
Renew: 9

Prayer for the Day / Collect
O God who created us for love: Grant us the wisdom to know that all you ask of us is for our good; through Jesus Christ our Savior. Amen.

OR

We come to worship God and to learn to follow Jesus more closely. We come to seek freedom even freedom from the things we love. Help us to seek the freedom that is real. Amen.

Prayer of Confession
Leader: Let us confess to God and before one another our sins and especially the ways in which we allow our possessions to enslave us.
People: We confess to you, O God, and before one another that we have sinned. We have received the good things you created for our pleasure and use and have made them our masters. There is almost nothing we

wouldn't do to acquire more and more stuff. Forgive our foolishness and open our eyes to the freedom you offer us to enjoy things without being owned by them. Amen.
Leader: God created us for love and relationships. God created things for our use and pleasure. May God grant us all the wisdom to sort this out.

Prayers of the People (and the Lord's Prayer)
We offer to you, O God, our praises and our worship, for you alone are the Holy One, you alone are God. We praise you for the love that is your essence and for your creative power.

(The following paragraph may be used if a separate prayer of confession has not been used.)
We confess to you, O God, and before one another that we have sinned. We have received the good things you created for our pleasure and use and have made them our masters. There is almost nothing we wouldn't do to acquire more and more stuff. Forgive our foolishness and open our eyes to the freedom you offer us to enjoy things without being owned by them.

We give you thanks for all the wonders of creation that you have set before us to use and enjoy. We thank you for the abundance of the earth that provides plenty for us to share. We thank you for the freedom you offer us to enjoy creation.

(Other thanksgivings may be offered.)
We offer to you the hurts and cares of your beloved creation. As you move among us bringing freedom and healing, help us to be part of your loving kindness.

(Other intercessions may be offered.)
All these things we ask in the name of our Savior Jesus Christ

who taught us to pray together saying:
Our Father... Amen.

(Or if the Lord's Prayer is not used at this point in the service)
All this we ask in the name of the Blessed and Holy Trinity.
Amen.

Proper 24
Pentecost 21
Ordinary Time 29

Job 38:1-7 (34-41)
Hebrews 5:1-10
Mark 10:35-45

Call to Worship
Leader: Let us bless God at all times.
People: God's praise shall continually be ours.
Leader: Our souls' boasts are in our God.
People: May the humble hear and be glad.
Leader: O magnify God with me.
People: Let us exalt God's name forever.

OR

Leader: God calls us to follow Jesus.
People: We have heard his call.
Leader: God calls us to serve as Jesus served.
People: We have found joy in serving others.
Leader: God calls us to be the world's slaves.
People: In this slavery we find freedom.

Hymns and Sacred Songs
"Make Me a Captive, Lord"
found in:
UMH: 421
PH: 378

"Lord, Speak to Me"
found in:

UMH: 463
PH: 426
NCH: 531

"Jesu, Jesu"
found in:
UMH: 432
H82: 602
PH: 367
NCH: 498
CH: 600
CCB: 66
Renew: 289

"Where He Leads Me"
found in:
UMH: 338
AAHH: 550
NNBH: 229
CH: 346

"Make Me a Servant"
found in:
CCB: 90

"We Are His Hands"
found in:
CCB: 85

Prayer for the Day / Collect
O God who comes in the form of a slave: Grant us the grace to follow your example and offer ourselves for others; through Jesus Christ our Savior. Amen.

OR

We come in awe that the very Son of God would come to serve us. In gratitude for this love we offer ourselves in service to others so that your love, O God, may be known throughout the earth. Amen.

Prayer of Confession

Leader: Let us confess to God and before one another our sins and especially the ways in which we seek to dominate others and get them to do our bidding.

People: We confess to you, O God, and before one another that we have sinned. We have seen how Jesus washed the disciples' feet and suffered and died. Yet we are so reluctant to take on the simple chores of helping others with their burdens. Forgive us our selfishness and so fill us with your Spirit that we may truly be servants for Jesus. Amen.

Leader: God comes to meet our needs so that we can have abundant and eternal life. God grant you forgiveness of sin and the time and desire to amend your lives.

Prayers of the People (and the Lord's Prayer)

We worship you as the One who reigns supreme over all creation and yet you come to us humble — as a servant. We are in awe of this kind of love.

(The following paragraph may be used if a separate prayer of confession has not been used.)

We confess to you, O God, and before one another that we have sinned. We have seen how Jesus washed the disciples' feet and suffered and died. Yet we are so reluctant to take on the simple chores of helping others with their burdens. Forgive us our selfishness and so fill us with your Spirit that we may truly be servants for Jesus.

We give you thanks for all that you have done to bring us into relationship with yourself and with others. There was no suffering and no task so lowly that you did not enter into it willingly to love us into life.

(Other thanksgivings may be offered.)
We pray for the world and its suffering. We pray for ourselves that we may truly reflect the serving love in which we were created. May your every word and act be a sign of your compassion and grace.

(Other intercessions may be offered.)
All these things we ask in the name of our Savior Jesus Christ who taught us to pray together saying:
Our Father... Amen.

(Or if the Lord's Prayer is not used at this point in the service)
All this we ask in the name of the Blessed and Holy Trinity. Amen.

Proper 25
Pentecost 22
Ordinary Time 30

Job 42:1-6, 10-17
Hebrews 7:23-28
Mark 10:46-52

Call to Worship
Leader: Let us exalt God's name together.
People: Our souls boast in God and are glad!
Leader: Look to God and be radiant!
People: In God we shall never be ashamed.
Leader: God's servants are redeemed!
People: In God's refuge we will never be condemned.

OR

Leader: Come and draw near for Jesus calls you.
People: With gladness we hear Jesus' voice.
Leader: He wants to grant you the desire of your hearts.
People: God's love is all that will satisfy us.
Leader: Jesus brings good news that we are loved by our God.
People: Thanks be to God! We have all we need.

Hymns and Songs
"Jesus Calls Us"
found in:
UMH: 398
H82: 549/550
NNBH: 183
NCH: 171/172

CH: 337
LBW: 494

"Lord, You Have Come to the Lakeshore" ("*Tu Has Venido a la Orilla*")
found in:
UMH: 344
PH: 377
CH: 342

"Come, All of You"
found in:
UMH: 350

"He Touched Me"
found in:
UMH: 367
AAHH: 273
NNBH: 147
CH: 564

"I Stand Amazed in the Presence"
found in:
UMH: 371

"Amazing Grace"
found in:
UMH: 378
H82: 671
PH: 280
AAHH: 271/272
NNBH: 161/162
NCH: 547/548
CH: 546

LBW: 448
Renew: 189

"This Is a Day of New Beginnings"
found in:
UMH: 383
NCH: 417
CH: 548

"Stand By Me"
found in:
UMH: 512
NNBH: 318
CH: 629

"I Will Call Upon the Lord"
found in:
CCB: 9
Renew: 15

"Your Loving Kindness Is Better than Life"
found in:
CCB: 26

Prayer for the Day / Collect
O God who comes by us in our hour of need: Grant us the faith to see that you have come to grant to us the only thing that can save us, even yourself; through Jesus Christ our Savior. Amen.

OR

We come to your sanctuary, O God, and bow ourselves before you. You are the source of all we need to be whole.

Open our eyes that we may see how much you love us and desire to heal us. Amen.

Prayer of Confession

Leader: Let us confess to God and before one another our sins and especially the ways we seek other things that cannot satisfy.

People: We confess to you, O God, and before one another that we have sinned. You ask what you can do for us and we begin to number the things we want: wealth, homes, jobs, good names. There really isn't anything wrong with the things that we desire except that we place them where only you belong. We forget that you are the only one who can satisfy the longings of our hearts. Forgive us and so fill us with your Spirit that we may truly seek you as the first in our lives so that we can truly enjoy the rest of your gifts to us. Amen.

Leader: God's great heart is full of love for us. God wants to satisfy the longing of our hearts by filling us with God's own Spirit.

Prayers of the People (and the Lord's Prayer)

We come to worship you, O God, who calls us from the brokenness of our lives and offers us wholeness and salvation.

(The following paragraph may be used if a separate prayer of confession has not been used.)

We confess to you, O God, and before one another that we have sinned. You ask what you can do for us and we begin to number the things we want: wealth, homes, jobs, good names. There really isn't anything wrong with the things that we desire except that we place them where only you belong. We forget that you are the only one who can satisfy the longings of our hearts. Forgive us and so fill us with your Spirit that we may truly seek you as the first in our lives so that we can truly enjoy the rest of your gifts to us.

We thank you for your steadfast love that comes to us in all the conditions of our lives and offers us hope and life eternal. We thank you for Jesus who has stopped and called us to you.

(Other thanksgivings may be offered.)
We pray for those who have not yet heard your call and for us who have heard it so imperfectly and answered it so hesitatingly.

(Other intercessions may be offered.)
All these things we ask in the name of our Savior Jesus Christ who taught us to pray together saying:
Our Father... Amen.

(Or if the Our Father is not used at this point in the service)
All this we ask in the name of the Blessed and Holy Trinity. Amen.

Reformation

Jeremiah 31:31-34
Romans 3:19-28
John 8:31-36

Call to Worship
Leader: God is our refuge and our strength.
People: God is a very present help in time of trouble.
Leader: We will not fear even if the earth changes.
People: We will not fear though the mountains shake.
Leader: The God of hosts is with us.
People: The God of Jacob is our refuge.

OR

Leader: Come and draw near to God.
People: We come with fear for we are not what we ought to be.
Leader: God already knows that and desires to transform our lives and reform our community.
People: We know we need to change. We trust in God's loving counsel.
Leader: Draw near to God and learn the truth.
People: We seek the truth for it will set us free.

Hymns and Sacred Songs
"A Mighty Fortress"
found in:
UMH: 110
H82: 687/688
PH: 200
AAHH: 124
NNBH: 374

NCH: 439/440
CH: 65
LBW: 228/229

"O Church of God, United"
found in:
UMH: 547

"The Church's One Foundation"
found in:
UMH: 545/546
H82: 525
PH: 442
AAHH: 337
NNBH: 297
NCH: 386
CH: 272
LBW: 369

"Forward Through the Ages"
found in:
UMH: 555
NCH: 377

"We Are the Church"
found in:
UMH: 558

"God of Grace and God of Glory"
found in:
UMH: 577
H82: 594/595
PH: 420
NCH: 436
CH: 464

LBW: 415
Renew: 301

"When the Church of Jesus"
found in:
UMH: 592
CH: 470

"Christ Loves the Church"
found in:
UMH: 590

"Our God Reigns"
found in:
CCB: 33

"Holy Ground"
found in:
CCB: 5

Prayer for the Day / Collect
O God who calls us into community: Grant us the faith to
trust you to help us reform our communities so that they may
reflect your reign and your love; through Jesus Christ our
Savior. Amen.

OR

You have called us, O God, into your presence so that we
might offer you our worship as you offer us your guidance
and salvation. Help us to be open to your love so that not
only our individual lives but our very communities might be
changed into your glory. Amen.

Prayer of Confession

Leader: Let us confess to God and before one another our sins and especially the ways we hang on to traditions that no longer work and deify our institutions.

People: We confess to you, O God, and before one another that we have sinned. There are things in our past that were helpful to us in knowing you and now we find that we cling to them as if they were what saved us and not you. Forgive us our foolishness and help us to open our lives to the fresh winds of your Spirit as you transform us and reform our institutions and communities. Amen.

Leader: God loves us and knows how difficult change can be for us. But God's love for us means that God wants us to grow and to grow up. Receive the love and forgiveness of God that will change us and make us better.

Prayers of the People (and the Lord's Prayer)

We worship and praise your Holy Name, O God, for you are our Creator and Redeemer. You constantly come to us to recreate us into your image.

(The following paragraph may be used if a separate prayer of confession has not been used.)

We confess to you, O God, and before one another that we have sinned. There are things in our past that were helpful to us in knowing you and now we find that we cling to them as if they were what saved us and not you. Forgive us our foolishness and help us to open our lives to the fresh winds of your Spirit as you transform us and reform our institutions and communities.

We give you thanks that you do not leave us alone to our own devices but come and offer us guidance and the very transformation of our beings. You will not rest until every person, every institution, every community has been reformed and brought into harmony with your reign.

(Other thanksgivings may be offered.)
We pray for ourselves and all creation as we are aware of how very far we are from your ideal for us. As you move among your creation seeking to redeem and claim each part, help us to not only offer ourselves for your reformation but to offer ourselves in helping others find the joy of living in your ways.

(Other intercessions may be offered.)
All these things we ask in the name of our Savior Jesus Christ who taught us to pray together saying:
Our Father....Amen.

(Or if the Our Father is not used at this point in the service)
All this we ask in the name of the Blessed and Holy Trinity. Amen.

All Saints

Wisdom of Solomon 3:1-9
Revelation 21:1-6a
John 11:32-44

Call to Worship
Leader: The earth is God's and all that is in it,
People: the world, and those who live in it;
Leader: for God has founded it on the seas
People: and established it on the rivers.
Leader: Who shall ascend the hill of God?
People: And who shall stand in God's holy place?
Leader: Those who have clean hands and pure hearts,
People: who do not lift up their souls to what is false, and do not swear deceitfully.
Leader: They will receive blessings from God
People: and vindication from the God of their salvation.

OR

Leader: Come and worship the God of all time.
People: We come and bow down to the God of eternity.
Leader: God's love and our place in it are never ending.
People: We rejoice in the God who is beyond time and death.
Leader: In God our sisters and brothers live forever.
People: There is no God like our God!

Hymns and Sacred Songs
"For All the Saints"
found in:
UMH: 711
H82: 287

PH: 526
AAHH: 339
NNBH: 301
NCH: 299
CH: 637
LBW: 174
ELA: 422

"Rejoice in God's Saints"
found in:
UMH: 708
CH: 476
ELA: 418

"I Sing a Song of the Saints of God"
found in:
UMH: 712
H82: 293
PH: 364
NCH: 295

"Hymn of Promise"
found in:
UMH: 707
NCH: 433
CH: 638

"Sing with All the Saints in Glory"
found in:
UMH: 702
ELA: 426

"In Christ There Is No East or West"
found in:
UMH: 548

H82: 529
PH: 439/440
AAHH: 398/399
NNBH: 299
NCH: 394/395
CH: 687
LBW: 259
ELA: 650

"Forward Through the Ages"
found in:
UMH: 555
NCH: 377

"I Love Thy Kingdom, Lord"
found in:
UMH: 540
H82: 524
PH: 441
NNBH: 302
NCH: 312
CH: 274
LBW: 368

"We Are One in Christ Jesus" ("*Somos uno en Cristo*")
found in:
CCB: 43

"The Steadfast Love of the Lord"
found in:
CCB: 28
Renew: 23

Prayer for the Day / Collect

O God who binds your children together eternally as the

body of Christ: Grant us the faith to trust ourselves and our loved ones to your never-failing love; through Jesus Christ our Savior. Amen.

OR

We have come to worship you, O God, for you are the one who has given us birth and who gives us life eternal through your own Spirit. You have united us as the body of Christ and we rejoice in our unity. May our worship be pleasing to you and our fellowship reflect your uniting love. Amen.

Prayer of Confession
Leader: Let us confess to God and before one another our sins and especially our failure to realize the presence of all God's saints.
People: We confess to you, O God, and before one another that we have sinned. We often feel sorry for ourselves because we think we are all alone. We imagine that no one suffers or has suffered as unjustly as we have suffered. We are so focused on ourselves that we forget our sisters and brothers who have lived in the faith through the ages. We are oblivious to their presence around us as they seek to encourage us. Forgives us our short sightedness and fill us with joy and gratitude for all your saints. Amen.
Leader: God delights in the communion of the saints as we care for one another. Receive the blessing of God as you appreciate once again the multitude of those who follow the path of Jesus with you.

Prayers of the People (and the Lord's Prayer)
We praise and glorify your name, O God, for you are the Eternal One who welcomes all into your life and reign. Your love is expansive and broad. Your grace is amazing and unending.

(The following paragraph may be used if a separate prayer of confession has not been used.)

We confess to you, O God, and before one another that we have sinned. We often feel sorry for ourselves because we think we are all alone. We imagine that no one suffers or has suffered as unjustly as we have suffered. We are so focused on ourselves that we forget our sisters and brothers who have lived in the faith through the ages. We are oblivious to their presence around us as they seek to encourage us. Forgive us our short sightedness and fill us with joy and gratitude for all your saints.

We give you thanks for all those who have died in the faith and continue to live with you and among us as the great cloud of witnesses. We thank you especially for... (here may be read the roll of the honored dead). You have blessed us with brothers and sisters in the faith who have held us in their prayers and have been beacons of light for us to better follow our Savior.

(Other thanksgivings may be offered.)

We pray for your creation, which groans for that time when salvation shall be complete. We pray for those who have not yet found you to be a loving, embracing God. We pray for ourselves that we might better reflect your love for your world.

(Other intercessions may be offered.)

All these things we ask in the name of our Savior Jesus Christ who taught us to pray together saying:
Our Father... Amen.

(Or if the Our Father is not used at this point in the service)

All this we ask in the name of the Blessed and Holy Trinity. Amen.

Proper 26
Pentecost 23
Ordinary Time 31

Ruth 1:1-18
Hebrews 9:11-14
Mark 12:28-34

Call to Worship
Leader: Let us praise God our whole life long!
People: We will sing praises to God as long as we live!
Leader: Happy are those whose hope is in the God of Jacob!
People: Our God, who made heaven and earth, keeps faith forever!
Leader: Our God watches over strangers.
People: Orphans and widows are in God's hands.

OR

Leader: Come and enter into God's way to eternal life.
People: What is that way that leads to life?
Leader: It is to love God with your whole being.
People: We will love God with our heart and soul.
Leader: It is to love your neighbor as yourself.
People: With God's help, we will love all those around us.

Hymns and Sacred Songs
"What Does the Lord Require?"
found in:
UMH: 441
H82: 605

PH: 405
CH: 659

"Seek Ye First"
found in:
UMH: 405
H82: 711
PH: 333
CH: 354

"Where Cross the Crowded Ways of Life"
found in:
UMH: 427
H82: 609
PH: 408
NCH: 543
CH: 665
LBW. 429

"Let There Be Peace on Earth"
found in:
UMH: 431
CH: 677

"More Love to Thee, O Christ"
found in:
UMH. 453
PH: 359
AAHH: 575
NNBH: 214
NCH: 456
CH: 527

"Lord, Speak to Me"
found in:

UMH: 463
PH: 426
NCH: 531

"My God, I Love Thee"
found in:
UMH: 470

"Near to the Heart of God"
found in:
UMH: 472
PH: 527
NNBH: 316
CH: 581

"Your Loving Kindness Is Better than Life"
found in:
CCB: 26

"I Am Loved"
found in:
CCB: 80

Prayer for the Day / Collect
O God who teaches your children the way of life: Grant
that we may have the faith to not only believe but to live by
the teachings of your blessed Son; through Jesus Christ our
Savior. Amen.

OR

We enter into your presence together this day, O God, to
praise you for your great love and wisdom. In love you
created us and in love you guide us into your life. Open our

hearts that we may not only hear the words of Jesus but that we might heed them, as well. Amen.

Prayer of Confession

Leader: Let us confess to God and before one another our sins and especially our reluctance to live what we believe.
People: We confess to you, O God, and before one another that we have sinned. We come to worship you and to hear your word for us yet we often leave just as we came. We say we believe you and we believe in you yet we are hesitant to actually turn our beliefs into actions. We claim Jesus as our Savior and Lord and yet we disregard his teachings. Forgive our hardhearted ways and send your Spirit upon us to steel our reserve to actually live as Christians and not just to talk like Christians. Amen.
Leader: God knows we are but the dust of the earth yet God continues to infuse us with the Spirit divine. Know that God loves us and calls us once again to the road to life.

Prayers of the People (and the Lord's Prayer)

We praise and worship you, O God, because you are our Creator and our Redeemer. You share your love and your life with your creatures.

(The following paragraph may be used if a separate prayer of confession has not been used.)
We confess to you, O God, and before one another that we have sinned. We come to worship you and to hear your word for us yet we often leave just as we came. We say we believe you and we believe in you yet we are hesitant to actually turn our beliefs into actions. We claim Jesus as our Savior and Lord and yet we disregard his teachings. Forgive our hardhearted ways and send your Spirit upon us to steel our reserve to actually live as Christians and not just to talk like Christians.

We give you thanks for all the ways in which you have blessed us and led us. You have given us your judges, seers, prophets, psalmists, and apostles. Most of all, you have given us yourself in Jesus Christ.

(Other thanksgivings may be offered.)
We pray for ourselves and all your children as we struggle to follow your way that leads to life. As you call all your people to yourself, help us to respond faithfully so that we may assist others in entering into your eternal life.

(Other intercessions may be offered.)
All these things we ask in the name of our Savior Jesus Christ who taught us to pray together saying:
Our Father... Amen.

(Or if the Our Father is not used at this point in the service)
All this we ask in the name of the Blessed and Holy Trinity. Amen.

Proper 27
Pentecost 24
Ordinary Time 32

Ruth 3:1-5; 4:13-17
Hebrews 9:24-28
Mark 12:38-44

Call to Worship
Leader: Unless God builds the house,
People: those who build it labor in vain.
Leader: Unless God guards the city,
People: the guard keeps watch in vain.
Leader: It is a vain thing to be anxious,
People: for God gives sleep to the beloved.

OR

Leader: We are called into the house of God.
People: Only in God's house do we find peace.
Leader: We are called into the city of God.
People: Only in God's city do we find security.
Leader: We are called into the family of God.
People: Only in God's family do we find real love.

Hymns and Sacred Songs
"Sing Praise to God Who Reigns Above"
found in:
UMH: 126
H82: 408
PH: 482
NCH: 6

CH: 6
Renew: 52

"God Will Take Care of You"
found in:
UMH: 130
AAHH: 137
NNBH: 52
NCH: 460

"All My Hope Is Firmly Grounded"
found in:
UMH: 132
H82: 665
NCH: 408
CH: 888

"Leaning on the Everlasting Arms"
found in:
UMH: 133
AAHH: 371
NNBH: 262
NCH: 471
CH: 56

"Rejoice, the Lord Is King"
found in:
UMH: 715/716
H82: 481
PH: 155
NCH: 303
CH: 699
LBW: 171

"How Majestic Is Your Name"
found in:
CCB: 21
Renew: 98

"The Steadfast Love of the Lord"
found in:
CCB: 28
Renew: 23

Prayer for the Day / Collect

O God who created us and keeps us day by day: Grant us the wisdom to understand that life comes from you and rests in you so that we may not be anxious but trust in your never-failing care; through Jesus Christ our Savior. Amen.

OR

We come to worship you, O God, and to pray for your presence in our midst. All that we do in worship and in service is but vain if you are not at the center of it. Keep us focused on you this morning and this week that we may find the peace and joy of being in your care. Amen.

Prayer of Confession

Leader: Let us confess to God and before one another our sins and especially the ways that we seek security and peace in things that cannot deliver either.

People: We confess to you, O God, and before one another that we have sinned. We have amassed all that is possible of the world's goods so that we will not be in want. Yet we are deeply aware that our needs have not been met. We have supported every effort of our nation to provide for our security, even when we were suspect of some of them. Yet we do not feel secure. We have gone

from relationship to relationship seeking love. Yet we do not feel loved. How foolish we are when all along you have been with us offering love, security, and that which truly satisfies. Forgive us and renew your Spirit within us that we may once again center our lives on you. Amen.

Leader: God desires to gather us as a hen gathers her chicks under her wing to care and love them. God grants us forgiveness and the presence of the Spirit that we may truly live in love, security, and peace, now and forever.

Prayers of the People (and the Lord's Prayer)
We worship and adore you, Creator and Sustainer of the universe, for the care with which you have made all that is and provided for its stability. As we learn more and more about the physical universe, we find ourselves in more awe at how it works. You are truly the awesome Creator.

(The following paragraph may be used if a separate prayer of confession has not been used.)
We confess to you, O God, and before one another that we have sinned. We have amassed all that is possible of the world's goods so that we will not be in want. Yet we are deeply aware that our needs have not been met. We have supported every effort of our nation to provide for our security, even when we were suspect of some of them. Yet we do not feel secure. We have gone from relationship to relationship seeking love. Yet we do not feel loved. How foolish we are when all along you have been with us offering love, security, and that which truly satisfies. Forgive us and renew your Spirit within us that we may once again center our lives on you.

We give you thanks for the ways in which you have sustained us and cared for us through the ages and through our lives. In the midst of flood, fire, storm, and war, you have always led us to a new future when we have been willing to follow. You have given us a resiliency that is amazing.

(Other thanksgivings may be offered.)
We pray to you for one another in our need and especially for those who are struggling and finding it difficult to trust in your care. We know how difficult it is to keep our eyes on what is important and how you sustain those things in the midst of the evil around us. Help us be a sign to others and a help to them that they may know of your never-failing love and care.

(Other intercessions may be offered.)
All these things we ask in the name of our Savior Jesus Christ who taught us to pray together saying:
Our Father... Amen.

(Or if the Lord's Prayer is not used at this point in the service)
All this we ask in the name of the Blessed and Holy Trinity. Amen.

Proper 28
Pentecost 25
Ordinary Time 33

1 Samuel 1:4-20
Hebrews 10:11-14 (15-18) 19-25
Mark 13:1-8

Call to Worship
Leader: My heart exults in God.
People: My strength is exalted in my God.
Leader: There is no Holy One like our God.
People: There is no rock like ours.
Leader: The bows of the mighty are broken.
People: But the feeble are girded in strength.

OR

Leader: God is our solid rock.
People: God is the eternal in the midst of the temporal.
Leader: God is our constant help in times of trouble.
People: Nothing separates us from the love of God.
Leader: We are God's beloved, now and forever.
People: We rejoice in the constant love of our God.

Hymns and Sacred Songs
"A Mighty Fortress Is Our God"
found in:
UMH: 110
H82: 687/688
PH: 260
AAHH: 124

NNBH: 37
NCH: 439/440
CH: 65
LBW: 228/229

"All My Hope Is Firmly Grounded"
found in:
UMH: 132
H82: 665
NCH: 408
CH: 88

"I Sing the Almighty Power of God"
found in:
UMH: 152
H82: 398
PH: 285
NCH: 12
Renew: 54

"How Firm a Foundation"
found in:
UMH: 529
H82: 636/637
PH: 361
AAHH: 146
NNBH: 48
NCH: 407
CH: 618
LBW: 507

"Leaning on the Everlasting Arms"
found in:
UMH: 133
AAHH: 371

NNBH: 262
NCH: 471
CH: 560

"O God, Our Help in Ages Past"
found in:
UMH: 117
H82: 680
AAHH: 170
NNBH: 46
NCH: 25
CH: 67
LBW: 320

"Source and Sovereign, Rock and Cloud"
found in:
UMH: 113
CH: 12

"The Care the Eagle Gives Her Young"
found in:
UMH: 118
NCH: 468
CH: 76

"On Eagle's Wings"
found in:
CCB: 97
Renew: 112

"All I Need Is You"
found in:
CCB: 100

Prayer for the Day / Collect

O God who is our solid rock: Grant us the wisdom to find in you the base for our lives that we may be firmly grounded in truth; through Jesus Christ our Savior. Amen.

OR

We come into your presence with thanksgiving and worship to find ourselves once again in the shadow of our solid rock. Refresh us and strengthen us that we may, without fear, trust ourselves to your eternal care and love. Amen.

Prayer of Confession

Leader: Let us confess to God and before one another our sins and especially the ways in which we substitute what is temporal for what is eternal.

People: We confess to you, O God, and before one another that we have sinned. We have taken the good things you have given us as signs of your eternal presence with us and treated them like they were what is really lasting. We have taken the good things of creation and gathered them around us as if they would be here forever. We have forgotten that you are the only One who is eternal. Forgive us our foolishness and grant us the power of your Spirit that we may once again center our lives in you. Amen.

Leader: God desires nothing more than our good. When we are ready to change the direction of our lives and look once more to the rock of our salvation, God welcomes us, forgives us, and gives us God's own Spirit.

Prayers of the People (and the Lord's Prayer)

We worship and adore you, O God, for you are the constant in a world that is ever changing. The things we thought were true have turned out to be false. The world we were born into is not the world we live in now. Yet you are always here bringing us your love and grace.

(The following paragraph may be used if a separate prayer of confession has not been used.)
We confess to you, O God, and before one another that we have sinned. We have taken the good things you have given us as signs of your eternal presence with us and treated them like they were what is really lasting. We have taken the good things of creation and gathered them around us as if they would be here forever. We have forgotten that you are the only One who is eternal. Forgive us our foolishness and grant us the power of your Spirit that we may once again center our lives in you.

We give you thanks for all that you have blessed us with in this life. When friends desert us, you are here. When our jobs, friends, or loved ones are taken from us, you are here. When our life seems meaningless, you are here. When our life seems over, you are here.

(Other thanksgivings may be offered.)
We bring to your loving care those who find themselves lost and without a firm place to stand. Some find their physical being failing. Some have lost their means of support. Some are lonely and grieving. Some are sick and dying. As you come and hold them in your never-failing arms enable us to reach out and share with them our physical image of your love and grace.

(Other intercessions may be offered.)
All these things we ask in the name of our Savior Jesus Christ who taught us to pray together saying:
Our Father... Amen.

(Or if the Lord's Prayer is not used at this point in the service)
All this we ask in the name of the Blessed and Holy Trinity.
Amen.

Thanksgiving Day

Joel 2:21-27
1 Timothy 2:1-7
Matthew 6:25-33

Call to Worship
Leader: Remember the goodness of God.
People: To think on God's goodness is like dreaming.
Leader: Let your mouths be filled with laughter.
People: Our tongues will shout for joy!
Leader: God has done great things for us!
People: May those who sow with tears, reap with joy!

OR

Leader: Come, let us give thanks to God for all we have received.
People: We are blessed beyond measure by our God.
Leader: Rejoice in the beauty and bounty of God's creation.
People: Such a creating God must be a God of great love.
Leader: God's love is ever around us if we would but perceive.
People: We will open our eyes to God's blessings and give God our thanks this day and all days.

Hymns and Sacred Songs
"All Creatures of Our God and King"
found in:
UMH: 62
H82: 400
PH: 455

AAHH: 147
NNBH: 33
NCH: 17
CH: 22
LBW: 527
Renew: 47

"Come, Ye Thankful People, Come"
found in:
UMH: 694
H82: 290
PH: 551
AAHH: 194
NNBH: 327
NCH: 422
CH: 718
LBW: 407

"For the Fruits of this Creation"
found in:
UMH: 97
H82: 424
PH: 553
NCH: 425
CH: 714
LBW: 562

"Now Thank We All Our God"
found in:
UMH: 102
H82: 396/397
PH: 555
NNBH: 330
NCH: 419

CH: 715
LBW: 533/534

"Praise to the Lord, the Almighty"
found in:
UMH: 139
H82: 390
AAHH: 117
NNBH: 2
NCH: 22
CH: 25
Renew: 57

"We Gather Together"
found in:
UMH: 131
H82: 433
PH: 559
NNBH: 326
NCH: 421
CH: 276

"Many and Great, O God"
found in:
UMH: 148
H82: 385
PH: 271
NCH: 3
CH: 58

"Praise, My Soul, the King of Heaven"
found in:
UMH: 66
H82: 410
PH: 478

CH: 23
LBW: 549
Renew: 53

"Give Thanks"
found in:
CCB: 92
Renew: 266

"For the Gift of Creation"
found in:
CCB: 67

Prayer for the Day / Collect
O God who created us and all creation out of your great love:
Grant us eyes of appreciation for all you have given us that
we might employ our tongues and our lives in thanksgiving;
through Jesus Christ our Savior. Amen.

OR

We praise you for your greatness, O God, and we thank you
for the blessings that come to us out of your loving kindness.
As we center ourselves into your worship and listen for your
voice give us thankful hearts that we may ever bless your
holy name. Amen.

Prayer of Confession
Leader: Let us confess to God and before one another our
sins and especially the ways in which we fail to give thanks
for all God's blessings to us.
**People: We confess to you, O God, and before one an-
other that we have sinned. We are truly blessed by your
love and kindness and yet we fail to give you thanks. We
act as if we were the ones who created the good earth and**

that we were the ones who made the crops to grow and the sun to shine. We look at the little we do to work with you and your creation and think we have done it all. Forgive us and fill us with appreciation and thanksgiving for all your blessings. Amen.

Leader: God never tires of blessing us or of hearing our thanksgiving. The love of God embraces us in our honest confession and empowers us to live as faithful disciples of Jesus.

Prayers of the People (and the Lord's Prayer)

Praise and glory and honor are yours, O God, for you are the Creator, Lover, and Redeemer of creation. You are the foundation of all that is and the giver of all good gifts.

(The following paragraph may be used if a separate prayer of confession has not been used.)
We confess to you, O God, and before one another that we have sinned. We are truly blessed by your love and kindness and yet we fail to give you thanks. We act as if we were the ones who created the good earth and that we were the ones who made the crops to grow and the sun to shine. We look at the little we do to work with you and your creation and think we have done it all. Forgive us and fill us with appreciation and thanksgiving for all your blessings.

We give you thanks for all the bounty of creation. The earth produces abundantly more than we could possibly image. You provide us not only with the necessities of life but with wondrous beauty as well. You are, indeed, a loving and giving God.

(Other thanksgivings may be offered.)
We pray for those who are deprived of your gifts by the greed and dishonesty of others. Some are denied food, shelter, freedom, education, and the very things that make life

possible. Some are denied love and care so that it is difficult for them to believe that anyone, even you, could be loving and kind. Help us to reach out in love so that they may believe you love them too.

(Other intercessions may be offered.)
All these things we ask in the name of our Savior Jesus Christ who taught us to pray together saying:
Our Father... Amen.

(Or if the Our Father is not used at this point in the service)
All this we ask in the name of the Blessed and Holy Trinity. Amen.

Christ the King
(Proper 29 / Ordinary Time 34)

2 Samuel 23:1-7
Revelation 1:4b-8
John 18:33-37

Call to Worship
Leader: Rise up, O God, and come to your dwelling place.
People: Let us worship you at your footstool.
Leader: Let your priests be clothed with righteousness,
People: and let your faithful shout for you.
Leader: God swore to David a sure oath that God will keep:
People: One of David's sons will sit on the throne forever.

OR

Leader: We come to celebrate the reign of our Christ.
People: We come as disciples of the Prince of Peace.
Leader: We come from a world of violence and death.
People: We come with grief and distress at the violence around us.
Leader: We come for a world from our Savior.
People: Lead us to your reign in these difficult times.

Hymns and Sacred Songs
"Let There Be Peace on Earth"
found in:
UMH: 431
CH: 677

"Crown Him with Many Crowns"
found in:
UMH: 327
H82: 494
PH: 151
AAHH: 288
NNBH: 125
NCH: 301
CH: 234
LBW: 170
Renew: 56

"Rejoice, the Lord Is King"
found in:
UMH: 715/716
H82: 481
PH: 155
NCII: 303
CII: 699
LBW: 171

"Ye Servants of God"
found in:
UMH: 181
H82: 535
PH: 477
NCH: 305
CH: 110
LBW: 252

"*Dona Nobis Pacem*"
found in:
UMH: 376
H82: 712

CH: 297
Renew: 240

"Majesty, Worship His Majesty"
found in:
UMH: 176
AAHH: 171
NNBH: 34
Renew: 63

"Hail to the Lord's Anointed"
found in:
UMH: 203
H82: 616
AAHH: 187
NCH: 104
CH: 140
LBW: 87
Renew: 101

"Jesus Shall Reign"
found in:
UMH: 157
H82: 544
PH: 423
NNBH: 10
NCH: 300
CH: 95
LBW: 530
Renew: 296

"Jesus, Name Above All Names"
found in:
CCB: 35
Renew: 26

"Our God Reigns"
found in:
CCB: 33

Prayer for the Day / Collect

O God who is our Creator and who has raised Jesus to reign over all in peace: Grant us the faith to trust that what is truly eternal is not power from violence but power from love; through Jesus Christ our Savior. Amen.

OR

We come to worship and acknowledge the Christ who rules over all. Even as we are aware of the power of evil and violence, we know that the Prince of Peace holds the true throne of love. Come and fill us with your peace, our Savior and our sovereign. Amen.

Prayer of Confession

Leader: Let us confess to God and before one another our sins and especially the ways in which we yield to the power of force and violence instead of the power of love and grace.
People: We confess to you, O God, and before one another that we have sinned. We call you our Savior and we have pledged to follow you but we cannot shake off the grip of violence and force as the true power. We listen to your teachings and then we insist on revenge while you offer forgiveness. We have lost sight of justice that heals and want only justice that punishes and destroys. Forgive us for betraying you and your ideals. Call us once more to be your peculiar people who find strength in love. Amen.
Leader: God has called us into the reign of Christ that we may be multiple signs of a new way of life. God welcomes all back into the fold and offers the power of the Holy Spirit to bring our intentions to reality.

Prayers of the People (and the Lord's Prayer)

We worship and adore you who reigns over all creation. We are in awe of your power and how you make that known in love and grace instead of terror and force.

(The following paragraph may be used if a separate prayer of confession has not been used.)

We confess to you, O God, and before one another that we have sinned. We call you our Savior and we have pledged to follow you but we cannot shake off the grip of violence and force as the true power. We listen to your teachings and then we insist on revenge while you offer forgiveness. We have lost sight of justice that heals and want only justice that punishes and destroys. Forgive us for betraying you and your ideals. Call us once more to be your peculiar people who find strength in love.

We give you thanks for the path Jesus offers us, which leads us away from the treadmill of violence and revenge to the true way of justice based on love and wholeness. We thank you for those who have followed Jesus faithfully and shown us the most excellent way.

(Other thanksgivings may be offered.)

We pray for all who suffer under the burden of violence and force. We pray for those who are abused in their homes, in their communities, or in their nations. We pray for those whose rights and lives are taken away through violence. We pray for those caught in the web of revenge that eats away at their very lives.

(Other intercessions may be offered.)

All these things we ask in the name of our Savior Jesus Christ who taught us to pray together saying:
Our Father... Amen.

(Or if the Lord's Prayer is not used at this point in the service)
All this we ask in the name of the Blessed and Holy Trinity.
Amen.

CPSIA information can be obtained
at www.ICGtesting.com
Printed in the USA
FFOW02n0620060916
27415FF